THE LIFE AND THOUGHT OF DAVID CRAIG

TEXTS AND STUDIES IN
PROTESTANT HISTORY AND THOUGHT IN QUEBEC

EDITORIAL BOARD

Richard Lougheed, *Institut de formation théologique de Montréal* and president, *Société d'histoire du protestantism franco-québécois*
Marie-Claude Rocher, *Institut sur le patrimoine culturel, Université Laval*, Quebec City, Quebec
A. Donald MacLeod, *Tyndale Theological Seminary*, Toronto, Ontario
Richard Vaudry, *The King's University College*, Edmonton, Alberta
Rob Clements, *Clements Academic*
Jean-Louis Lalonde, *Société d'histoire du protestantisme franco-québécois*
Jason Zuidema, *McGill University* and *Farel Reformed Theological Seminary*, Montreal, Quebec

VOLUMES

Vol. 1—*The Controversial Conversion of Charles Chiniquy*, Richard Lougheed, 2008.

Vol. 2—*The Life and Thought of David Craig (1937–2001): Canadian Presbyterian Missionary*, Jason Zuidema, 2008.

The Life and Thought of David Craig

1937–2001
Canadian Presbyterian Missionary

JASON ZUIDEMA

CLEMENTS ACADEMIC
TORONTO

THE LIFE AND THOUGHT OF DAVID CRAIG
Copyright © 2008 Jason Zuidema

Published 2008 by
CLEMENTS PUBLISHING
6021 Yonge St., Box 213
Toronto, Ontario M2M 3W2 Canada
www.clementspublishing.com

All rights reserved. No part of this publication may be reproduced, stored in a retrieval system, or transmitted, in any form or by any means, electronic, mechanical, photocopying, recording or otherwise, without the prior permission of the publisher or the Copyright Licensing Agency.
\

Library and Archives Canada Cataloguing in Publication

Zuidema, Jason, 1978-
The life and thought of David Craig (1937–2001): Canadian Presbyterian missionary / Jason Zuidema.

Includes bibliographical references.
ISBN 978-1-894667-94-4

1. Craig, David, 1937-2001. 2. Presbyterian Church in Canada—Missions. 3. Missionaries—Canada—Biography. 4. Clergy—Québec (Province)—Biography. I. Title.

BV3705.C73Z83 2008   266'.023710092   C2008-906603-0

To young Christians throughout *la belle province*

Contents

Preface ix

Part I—The Life of David Craig

Chapter 1: Parents, Siblings, Missionaries
          and Brethren 3
Chapter 2: Clinging to Presbyterianism and
          the Attraction of a Klinck 11
Chapter 3: Missionaries! 29
Chapter 4: "The Longest Moment of
          David Craig" By Ernest Hillen............................41
Chapter 5: Alive..53
Chapter 6: A Story to Tell...59
Chapter 7: A Student Again...71
Chapter 8: Evangelism and the Église
          Catholique Réformée...79
Chapter 9: United and Divided 99
Chapter 10: Slowing Down and Moving Forward 125
Chapter 11: At Rest 135

Part II—The Thought of David Craig

Chapter 12: A Missionary's Theology 147
Chapter 13: "A Dialogue about Dialogue"
       in *Presbyterian College Life* (1965) 167
Chapter 14: "The Protestant Witness in Quebec" (c. 1981) 171
Chapter 15: "The Power of the Spirit" in *Parole* (1985) 179
Chapter 16: "Remember the Days of Old"
       in *Canada's Huguenot Heritage* (1987) 185
Chapter 17: "An Interview with David Craig"
       in *Channels* (1988) 193
Chapter 18: "The First Mark of the Church" 201

Bibliography 207
Index 223

Preface

I met David Craig for the first time almost ten years ago. I had been invited by several pastors in the *Église Réformée du Québec* to observe a synod meeting which was being held at the Craig home in Repentigny. I left Montreal mid-afternoon on a Friday with three other delegates and made what seemed like an interminably long drive only to arrive an hour too early at David's house. We apologized for our early arrival, but David thought nothing of it. As a young theological student, I was fairly nervous being in the company of pastors, and synodical meetings had always seemed to me to be extremely formal affairs. This conception, however, was quickly broken as David ushered us into the swimming pool area at the back of his house and urged us to put on the swimming trunks he had readily available for guests. For the next half hour we spent time floating, splashing and diving like a bunch of schoolboys. I almost forgot why we had come in the first place.

These were my first impressions of David Craig: a man who would welcome a stranger into his home, a man who would play with childlike delight, a man who could be serious and reverent during the meeting that followed. I met him on several later occasions and heard him preach a number of times, but never really had the opportunity to study under him or work alongside him. I regret that I did not have much time to get to know the man better during his life. So I have had to content myself with what I have learned in this last year rereading everything I could find about him. I can say that it has been a pleasure getting to know him more fully, even if I am a little late.

One of the most memorable moments came when I was rereading a sermon on '*bilans*' for the New Year.[1] I was present for this sermon on the last Sunday of the year 2000, but I had not yet learned the French word '*bilan*'. Hence, when David said that we all made them, I ought to have one, the Bible spoke about them, etc., I was not quite sure what to think. In any case, it was good to finally figure out that David was calling his congregation to give an honest 'assessment' of their lives before God in the year 2000 and to continue to live their lives before God in 2001.

It would be false to say that the following work is entirely 'objective' historical research. Yet it would be equally false to say any historian's work is entirely 'objective'. Every historian writes with a certain bias and for certain purposes. Thus, it is important for me to note my biases and purposes at the outset. This book will not be a work of hagiography—the praise of 'Saint' David Craig. David would have been the first to criticise himself and his own weaknesses. He was only one among many important missionaries and workers in Nigeria, Switzerland and Quebec. Several of these other people have already been the subjects of biographies or are found in history books, and one hopes the many others will also one day be noted for their contributions. In particular, the other participants involved in the formation of the *Alliance Réformée Évangélique* (A.R.E.) or the *Conseil des Églises Réformées du Québec* (C.E.R.Q.) in the mid-1980s do not figure prominently enough beside David in this work. Their important stories ought to be written in the coming years.

Although David experienced many adventures and joyful moments during his lifetime, he also participated in situations that tore apart relationships and were a source of disappointment for him and others.

---

1. Sermon 453: "La production en 2001!"

SURVEYING THE LANDSCAPE

I have tried to be as balanced in my presentation of both the joyful and the difficult times as the sources will allow.

I must confess, however, that I do think David was in many ways a model Christian pastor. Whether or not we knew him, I think his life story ought to be told to remind us of the joys and struggles in Christian ministry in the second half of the 20th century. The story will be based on the available sources—written, printed or eyewitness accounts. Throughout, I have been careful to base judgments on these sources (a complete listing is found in the bibliography at the end of this work). This book is not meant to be an exhaustive biography of David Craig. If there are particular stories about David that ought to have made it into the book, please share them with others who are reading the book. I hope this book will be a conversation starter and not a conversation stopper.

Gathering these sources would not have been possible without the work of Nancy and David for the last five decades. Much of David's written legacy was given by Nancy to the archives of the Eglise Réformée St-Paul shortly after David's passing in 2001.[2] David's sermons came in three large boxes and were in no particular order. In order to keep them straight, I numbered the French sermons 1-797 and the English sermons E1-E102. Often David used interesting stories or memories from his own life to help make a point in a sermon. These details have proved invaluable in writing this biography.

Further detail about David's life and thought was found in his other notes, handouts and presentations. I refer to them by their title or other information if possible. For photos and letters, Nancy generously allowed me to rummage through a number of boxes of precious memories. These, again, I refer to by title or date where possible. I obtained many of the other manuscripts and published documents

---

2. Although most papers in this archival collection can be identified by author and date, there were a number that could not be fully identified. I have supplied some supplementary information in square brackes when possible, but some references are still incomplete.

XI

in the archives and library of The Presbyterian College, Montreal, the library of Farel Reformed Theological Seminary and the Records and Archives Office of the Presbyterian Church in Canada located in Toronto, Ontario.

It is astounding to note how many people helped in writing this biography. I thank all those who graciously and patiently accorded me their time on one or numerous occasions. I thank in particular Nancy Craig. I also thank, in no particular order, Dr. Daniel Racine, Mr. John Miller, Mr. Archie McLean, Dr. Mike Pettem, Rev. Ross Davidson, Rev. Jean-Guy deBlois, Rev. Jean Zoellner, Rev. Dr. John Vissers, Rev. Dr. Daniel Shute, Rev. Dr. Hans Kouwenberg, Mr. Jim Craig, Mr. Dick Craig, Rev. Dr. Ian Rennie, Ms. Kit Schindell, Rev. Laurence Mawhinney, Rev. Paul Scott, Rev. Dr. A. Donald MacLeod, Rev. Dr. Harold Kallemeyn, Ms. Rosemary Walker, Rev. Blake Walker, Mr. Paul Reader, Mr. Fred Nichols, Rev. Erich Brunner, Dr. Richard Lougheed and Rev. Paulin Bédard. I thank Mr. Bob Anger of the Presbyterian Church Archives, Toronto, for his willingness to help find documents relating to this project and for having them ready for perusal when I came to the Archives for an all-too-brief visit during my research. Further, I thank all other individuals to whom I asked questions about David for this project.

I thank several individuals and organizations for allowing me to reproduce certain articles by or about David in this volume. My gratitude goes to Ernest Hillen and the *Montreal Gazette* for their permission to reprint "The Longest Moment of David Craig." I am also grateful to John Vissers and The Presbyterian College, Montreal, for the permission to reprint David's articles, "A Dialogue about Dialogue" and "Protestant Witness in Quebec." Thanks too, to Calvin Brown, the editor of *Channels* magazine, a publication of The Renewal Fellowship within The Presbyterian Church in Canada, for permission to reproduce "An Interview with David Craig." Thank you to the Ontario Genealogical Society, the current administrators of the archives of the Huguenot Society of Canada, for permission to reproduce "Remember the Days of Old." Finally, I thank the Rev. Jean-Guy deBlois, administrator of the A.R.E.-Farel, for permission to reproduce the article "The Power of the Spirit."

Many individuals helped with encouragement, in editing, in technical matters, in typing/scanning documents or in translating (this book has been launched simultaneously in English and French). For work on typing David's notes, locating documents and translating texts, I thank Ms. Christiane Rousseau (Fichault), Ms. Sylvie Lebrun (Sparks), Dr. Daniel Racine, Mr. Marc-André Pigeon, Rev. Bernard Westerveld, Mr. David Rozeboom, Mr. Philippe deBlois, Ms. Erin Zoellner and Ms. Amy Ballor. I thank Dr. Daniel Timmer for generously allowing me to have office space in his home for several months to read and write.

Financing for this project came from several very generous individuals and organizations who stipulated that proceeds from the book continue to serve mission and Christian education in Quebec. The Priscilla and Stanford Reid Trust, a foundation which supports reformed and presbyterian theological education projects in Canada, generously designated funds for the translation of this book into French.

Continual encouragement during the research for and writing of this project came from my family (especially my wife Anna and my children Geneviève and Kaleb) and my church community. I quietly worked on this project in my spare time for the better part of a year and am pleased I can finally present it to them. Originally, my goal in writing this book was to provide a model of sorts for the young Christians in my church to help them form their identity as Christians. Since many young French-speakers are first or second generation members of evangelical churches, they often lack such models. Throughout the project this goal has not changed. It is for this reason that I dedicate this book to all the young Christians growing up in *la belle province*.

Above all, I thank God from whom all blessings flow.

PART I

The Life of David Craig

trator of the A.R.E.-Farel, for permission to reproduce the article "The Power of the Spirit."

Many individuals helped with encouragement, in editing, in technical matters, in typing/scanning documents or in translating (this book has been launched simultaneously in English and French). For work on typing David's notes, locating documents and translating texts, I thank Ms. Christiane Rousseau (Fichault), Ms. Sylvie Lebrun (Sparks), Dr. Daniel Racine, Mr. Marc-André Pigeon, Rev. Bernard Westerveld, Mr. David Rozeboom, Mr. Philippe deBlois, Ms. Erin Zoellner and Ms. Amy Ballor. I thank Dr. Daniel Timmer for generously allowing me to have office space in his home for several months to read and write.

Financing for this project came from several very generous individuals and organizations who stipulated that proceeds from the book continue to serve mission and Christian education in Quebec. The Priscilla and Stanford Reid Trust, a foundation which supports reformed and presbyterian theological education projects in Canada, generously designated funds for the translation of this book into French.

Continual encouragement during the research for and writing of this project came from my family (especially my wife Anna and my children Geneviève and Kaleb) and my church community. I quietly worked on this project in my spare time for the better part of a year and am pleased I can finally present it to them. Originally, my goal in writing this book was to provide a model of sorts for the young Christians in my church to help them form their identity as Christians. Since many young French-speakers are first or second generation members of evangelical churches, they often lack such models. Throughout the project this goal has not changed. It is for this reason that I dedicate this book to all the young Christians growing up in *la belle province*.

Above all, I thank God from whom all blessings flow.

PART I

The Life of David Craig

CHAPTER ONE

Parents, Siblings, Missionaries and Brethren

DAVID'S CHILDHOOD

Although he often cited a date one or two years later, David Trevor Craig was born on 28 December 1937.[1] His family lived in Brantford, Ontario, until his father, Trevor, was drawn to Guelph, Ontario, in 1945 to teach beekeeping at the Ontario Agricultural College.

Trevor and David's mother, Ruth, loved children and soon David, the eldest child, had ten younger siblings whom he could affectionately pester.[2] With Jim (James), Dick (Richard), Muriel, Evan, Sylvia,

---

1. In documents studied for this book, I came across the dates 1937, 1938 and 1939 for David's birth. For example, in the material from the Board of World Missions of The Presbyterian Church in Canada, his birth date is listed as December 1938. More impressive is an official *'Curriculum vitae'* from later in his life which lists his date of birth as 28 December 1939! The best, however, is a story from the treasurer of David's church in Trois-Rivières who confirmed that on all official documents from his tenure there, his birth date was 28 December 1938. Finally, his friends in Quebec celebrated his 60th birthday in December 1998! For David these date changes were not so much a lie as they were a really good practical joke.

2. In Sermon 638 he fondly remembers his large family.

Paul, Fred, Bill (William), Mark and Ian, there was always something happening in the Craig house.

Nurturing the first few children in the latter years of the Depression was not an easy task for Trevor and Ruth. The Craig family was not wealthy, but what they lacked in riches, they made up for in the quality of their family relations. With limited financial resources, the children had to be content with hand-me-downs. Many items, from clothes to shoes and even skates were passed from David to the others. The thirteen family members also shared a big house with a generous garden that provided them with an abundant array of fresh vegetables and fruits. Of course, it also provided them with a multitude of chores as well; with a large family and a large house, there was always plenty of work to do!

The Craigs, however, also knew how to have fun. They spent a lot of time together, and with no television or video games to occupy their time, the children had to use their imaginations to provide their own entertainment. For example, they always had enough players for a baseball game! David, being the oldest, was naturally captain of one of the teams.

In addition to being captain, David's place as the eldest sibling also meant he was served first at the mealtime. Since milk and dessert were laid out before dinner began at the Craig home, David always had his choice of the first and biggest piece and would often try to barter it to one of his brothers or sisters for something more valuable to him. His siblings affectionately referred to him as "the garbage man" because he would eat anything they did not want to eat on their plates.

Holidays were an especially exciting time in the Craig household. On Christmas morning, everyone was eager to receive the gifts in their stockings. One gift in particular, from Aunt Jean in Montreal, was always anticipated with much excitement. Aunt Jean had a special place in her heart for the Craig children and would always send an enormous package. Once she sent David a pair of skis for Christmas. On another occasion the family gift was a long toboggan with six seats. These gifts provided a lot of family fun and created lasting memories.

PARENTS, SIBLINGS, MISSIONARIES AND BRETHREN

Another memory that dominated David's childhood was beekeeping, which he learned from his father. Growing up, David and his two oldest siblings worked a great deal with the bees. They were often responsible for tending the hives at home and selling the honey at the Guelph market. Sometimes they would go door-to-door selling honey to their neighbours for a certain cut of the total profit. David recalls his father's interest in beekeeping with great fondness:

> My father was a bee-keeper in his spare time. It was an activity that he loved to do. Often he would take me and my brother with him out into the country to see the progress of his hives. We never had the impression that he made an effort to give us these few moments with him. He took us as companions to participate in something interesting. It was a natural and spontaneous way to include us in his activities.[3]

David eventually followed in his father's footsteps and developed a life-long interest in beekeeping.[4] Not only did it provide him with many hours of pleasure, but he used it in his work as a pastor, referring often to the theological significance of the well-run hive.[5]

David went to public school in Brantford until 1945 when the family moved to Guelph and he transferred to MacDonald Consolidated School, which was very close to the Ontario Agricultural College.[6] Every day he and his brothers would make the quarter-mile trek to and

---

3. Sermon 74.
4. In her letters to friends of May 1980 and June 1982, Nancy noted David's continuing love of beekeeping and how it was a healthy distraction for him.
5. Sermons 87, 201 and 665.
6. MacDonald Consolidated was built in 1904 as a model school amalgamating small rural schools into one larger school with qualified teachers, an initiative known as the 'MacDonald Movement'. Funding was provided by Sir William MacDonald, a Montreal tobacco manufacturer and philanthropist who believed this consolidation was the wisest way to build for the future. The school closed in 1972 and reopened as The MacDonald Stewart Art Centre.

from school. Most often the walks gave the boys time for playful banter, but they also had their fair share of fights.

For high school David attended Guelph Collegiate and Vocational Institute.[7] He did not receive the highest marks of his class, but was nonetheless quite gifted. His teachers remarked that his problem was one of lack of effort, not capacity. Once he became interested in a subject, his grades rose dramatically. In fact—and this is ironic considering his later career—this lack of effort was most pointed out in his French courses. Considering his grade nine French grades, no one would have expected that David Craig would end his adult life immersed in French.[8]

Apart from studying and being with his friends, David kept busy with part-time jobs. In addition to beekeeping and delivering papers, David worked at a local bakery. On Saturdays he drove truck for The Guthrie Bakery (owned by Frank Guthrie, a senior elder and lay preacher at Eramosa Gospel Hall) delivering baked goods to the bakery's various stores. With the money he made from his various jobs, he and his brothers 'invested' in a 1926 Model-T Ford. The car was not fancy, but it was much more fun and efficient than walking. Because of the configuration of the car's gas tank it was often difficult to go up hills if the tank was near empty, so David and his brothers would often have to slowly back up a hill in order to drive down the other side.

SPIRITUAL GROWTH AND CHOICES FOR THE FUTURE

Trevor and Ruth spent a great deal of time nurturing their children to be strong Christian citizens. While in Brantford, the Craigs attended a

---

7. GCVI is one of the oldest continuously operating high schools in the province of Ontario. During the years David studied there the buildings showed signs of aging. In 1962 some of the older buildings (presumably in which David had studied) were torn down to facilitate several more additions including a modern gym, business and science wing and tech wings.

8. See David's "Student's Report," Guelph Collegiate Vocational Institute, 1952–53.

Brethren assembly and then joined the Eramosa Gospel Hall when they moved to Guelph. The Brethren movement began in the 19th century and was based on a general dissatisfaction with established Protestant churches and a desire to return to the perceived simplicity of worship and church order in the New Testament.[9] Within the movement certain congregations were more resistant than others to working with other evangelical churches. Although the Eramosa Gospel Hall had once been more closed to such fellowship, they had more recently cultivated more positive relationships with 'established' churches.[10]

It was in this small Christian assembly that David learned the basics of the Christian faith and a warm Christian devoutness.[11] On Sundays David would go with his family to the 'breaking of bread' service at 11 a.m., Sunday school at 3 p.m. and again with his father and older brothers to the evening gospel service. At home David and his siblings

---

9. The Eramosa Gospel Hall was for several generations an 'exclusive' Brethren assembly in the vein of F.W. Grant (1834–1902), a famous English Brethren teacher. In the 19th century a division occurred among the Brethren dividing the 'open' from the 'exclusive.' Open Brethren taught that they could receive to the Lord's Supper any believer who was personally sound in faith, even though the congregation or assembly from which he came might harbour erroneous teaching. The exclusive Brethren, however, "regarded the 'separation from evil as God's principle of unity' and held that to receive to the Lord's Supper a brother from an assembly in which error is taught, even though he might personally reject it, disqualified the receiving assembly from participation in what often came to be called the 'Circle of Fellowship.'" Arthur Carl Piepkorn, "Plymouth Brethren (Christian Brethren)," *Concordia Theological Monthly* 41 (1970): 165.

10. In the 1940s and 50s, the 'Grant' assemblies moved increasingly toward an 'open' position. The Eramosa Gospel Hall, therefore, was no exception to this rule. See Piepkorn, "Plymouth Brethren," 168; F.R. Coad, *A History of the Brethren Movement: Its Origins, Its Worldwide Development and Its Significance for the Present Day* (Vancouver: Regent College Publishing, 2001).

11. For example, David would always appreciate the life and teaching of the Brethren preacher George Müller of Bristol. See Arthur T. Pierson, *George Müller of Bristol* (London: James Nisbet, 1901).

were encouraged by their parents to read the Bible and pray. David's father also led a family devotion time at supper every day.

When David became a teenager, he began to do some deep spiritual searching. One particular Sunday while coming home from a church meeting, he turned to his brother Jim and remarked that he had asked that day for the Lord to be his Saviour. This was an incredibly important step in David's life. Although he was from a strong Christian family, David knew that he did not simply inherit true faith. His family was Christian to the fifth generation, but he too needed the grace of God and the gift of faith by the Holy Spirit. Faith, said David later in life, was never simply 'natural' but always a gift.[12] Because of David's testimony, Jim also responded to the Lord's call that day.

Although David's life path was not yet clear, he knew he wanted to follow it as a child of the Lord. As a teenager, David developed an interest in missions. Often his parents would invite visiting missionaries to stay at their home, which provided David the opportunity to learn from missionaries who worked out in the field. As he reflected on his life more deeply, it was only natural that he would start thinking about these more serious things.[13]

In high school David was an enthusiastic participant in activities on campus, including the school's Bible club. The club would customarily invite a special speaker to share some thoughts and lead a prayer time, but sometimes David himself would lead the meditation on a verse from Scripture. He seemed, even back then, to have a gift for talking about his faith. It was a gift that would lead him throughout his ministry.

After graduation, David started work at the Royal Bank of Canada, quickly moving up the employment ladder from teller to assistant manager in a short period of time. Obviously he was a keen worker, but he too strongly felt the call to mission work to remain at the bank.[14] Often those who are surrounded by mission-oriented folk (or are

---

12. Sermon 30.
13. Sermon 30.
14. Sermon E97.

children of missionaries) soon feel the call to missions themselves.[15] A normal option for a young man from a Brethren background interested in missions was to study at Chicago's Emmaus Bible College or Toronto Bible College—but David followed another route.

It was unusual for a young man from a Brethren milieu (even if it was now of the 'Open' variety) to study at an organized mainline church school, but David nonetheless chose this direction. Support for this venture came from Frank Guthrie, who himself had been raised Presbyterian and became acquainted with Christian Brethren fundamentalism in Toronto around the time of World War I.[16] Mr. Guthrie, for whom David worked at The Guthrie Bakery, was a leader in the local Brethren assembly and had a clear vision for missions. He encouraged David to pursue the service of the Lord. After some discussions and prayer, David's parents also encouraged him to take up formal studies. Knowing he had their spiritual support, David enrolled in the pre-theology program at Waterloo Lutheran University.[17]

---

15. See Jeanne Stevenson Moessner, "Missionary Motivation," *Sociological Analysis* 53/2 (1992): 189–201.

16. For more on Frank Guthrie's preaching and mission work see: David A. Martin, "Mennonite Fundamentalism and the Hawkesville Brethren: an examination of the origins of the Wallenstein Bible Chapel and its impact on the local Mennonite Community," *Waterloo Historical Society* 91 (2004).

17. David's father was fairly open to other denominations' mission work as a legitimate expression of God's kingdom work. In fact, he later gave his boys the book *Brethren Hang Loose* by Robert C. Girard (Zondervan, 1972), which promoted a more broad-minded and flexible structure in church practice to renew evangelical churches.

CHAPTER TWO

Clinging to Presbyterianism and the Attraction of a Klinck

UNIVERSITY DAYS

With big dreams of serving the Lord, David was off to university at Waterloo College of Arts in Waterloo, Ontario. Although it was not far from his home, his university experience formed opinions and relationships which would influence the rest of his life. David had lots of time during his university years to enjoy student life, but he also took ideas and thoughtful conversation very seriously. During his years of study his faith in the Lord was anchored even more firmly, yet he was exposed to and embraced a different form of Christianity than he had known.

Waterloo College of Arts was affiliated with the University of Western Ontario until 1960, when it revised its charter to be independent and changed its name to Waterloo Lutheran University.[1] At this university there was a pre-theological track for students wishing to

---

1. In 1973 the university dropped its church affiliation with the Evangelical Lutheran Church and changed its name again to Wilfred Laurier University in order to receive provincial funding.

study at a seminary after university studies. Although the school was officially Lutheran, students from all denominations were encouraged to study there. In fact, as well as the non-denominational InterVarsity Christian Fellowship, there were also various denominational clubs for pre-theological students.

David took full advantage of these campus clubs. He frequented both the InterVarsity Christian Fellowship and the Presbyterian students' Westminster Club. In the Westminster Club, in particular, David got to know more about the Presbyterian tradition and the Presbyterian Church. For him, much of this history was new. With several of his fellow club participants, Paul Scott among others, David had long discussions about the Reformers, the Westminster Confession and the history of Presbyterianism in Europe and North America. David, being from a Brethren background, was particularly impressed with the larger and longer vision of Presbyterianism and its confessions and ordered ministry. He did not reject outright his Brethren past, but he did see it as lacking depth and precision. Gradually, in conversation with others in the club, David became convinced of the biblical foundation for practices such as ordination.[2] Through his involvement with this group he sharpened his abilities as a theological thinker and prepared his mind for seminary.

In addition to the various clubs, David's classroom education taught him to think critically about some of the more pressing theological questions of his day. Significantly, David studied under historian, lawyer and apologist John Warwick Montgomery. Professor Montgomery helped David think about the absolute centrality of the crucifixion and resurrection of Jesus Christ. David relates the story of how Montgomery walked into the classroom on the first day of the semester and drew a giant cross on the board marking the central point in history.[3]

---

2. Later in life David would highly praise the 'beauty' of the Reformed system of ordination and church government. He argued that it was the best system to ensure a stable and unified leadership. Sermon 710.

3. Sermons 188, 498, 579, 640, E37, E94.

David appreciated Montgomery's definition of history as "the hand of God in the dealings of man."[4] Further, Montgomery's emphasis that the Christian faith is based on historical fact was heartily shared by David.[5] For the first number of years as a preacher David clearly called his listeners to faith not *in spite of* the facts, but *because of* the facts.[6] On one occasion David stated:

> God does not ask us to believe despite the facts! He asks us to believe because of the facts. To have faith is not to force oneself to believe the impossible, but rather to rely on God because of what he has done in time and space in Jesus Christ. Faith is our profound and personal commitment to follow Jesus Christ.[7]

Throughout his career David highlighted the trustworthiness of Scripture, but he himself confessed that in later years he moved away from the fact-centred preaching he had learned as a student to a greater emphasis on the presence of Christ and the joy of the Christian life.[8] Even with this change of emphasis, the facts of Scripture and the facts of Christian history were still imperative to his beliefs throughout ministry.[9]

---

4. "L'Histoire est la main de Dieu dans les affaires de l'homme." Sermon 498.

5. David kept an unpublished manuscript given out by Montgomery in class entitled: "The Quest for Absolutes: an Historical Argument." The paper clearly argues for the reliability and defensibility of biblical history. Notably, the paper contends that in these sorts of arguments one needs to examine one's presuppositional footings.

6. For example: Sermons 139, 238, 422, 602, 711.

7. Sermon 238 [translation mine].

8. Sermon 27.

9. Biblical history and Reformation history often went hand-in-hand in David's preaching and teaching. In sermon 63, for example, David linked the objective reality of the Huguenot Gaspard de Coligny, one of the figures to which French Protestantism owes its existence, with the objective reality of the resurrection, the figure to which all Christians owe their existence. David was concerned that one forgets neither of these facts.

David's friends remember with fondness the years they spent at university together. They remember David Craig as a young man with a generous spirit, a deep joy and a quirky sense of humour. Half-way through his first year, David moved into a small basement apartment made for students with his friend Paul Reader. The owners of the house had recently remodelled and, for unknown reasons, had put two toilets (with no divisions) into the apartment washroom. David and Paul made the best of this weird arrangement by setting up a chess game on a small table between the toilets. When either felt the call of nature, he would take his place on his private throne and also make his next move in the ongoing chess game.

Further, David's friends recount many stories that exemplify his lovable gullibility. A few examples should suffice:

David's mother was a talented baker and occasionally she would bring desserts for David and his roommates to eat. Often while David was showing his parents out, his roommates would storm the kitchen to check out the baked treats. By the time David got back to the kitchen, much of what his mother had just brought over had already been eaten. It became so important to get that last piece of pie that one time after church David rushed back to the house to stake his claim. In his wonderful green suit he hurried into the kitchen to find that there was indeed one piece left for him. Victoriously he went outside to parade his piece of pie in front of his friends, but in his haste he stumbled and the pie ended up all over his suit.

On another occasion David was living in the manse of a local Presbyterian Church with Paul and another friend named Archie McLean. One day when David was getting on Archie and Paul's nerves, they went into the sanctuary of the church and tied David to one of the fancy and expensive chairs commonly found in the front of older Presbyterian church sanctuaries. With David tied to the chair, Archie and Paul lugged him three blocks away and left him alone in the middle of the city's main intersection. About forty-five minutes later David came sauntering into the house free from his chains. His roommates were very concerned about this—not because David was free, but because the expensive church chair was still sitting in the middle of the intersection! (They went immediately to retrieve it.) All in all, his classmates and roommates recall that David took their practical jokes with a great deal of fun.

Finally, David and his roommates were (in)famous for 'borrowing' the Waterloo Lutheran University mascot for a short time in early 1961. Many at the university were very disturbed about the disappearance of their beloved 'goldenhawk'. Most suspected that it was a malicious attempt by a rival university to tarnish their good name. To add fuel to the fire, David had his picture taken in the suit of the mascot as a sort of ransom photo for the local paper.[10] The prank was over, however, when people identified the mascot's fairly distinctive shoes as David's. In the end, David had to explain his actions before the student council.

During his time at Waterloo, David not only made time for fun, but he also made it a point to be a more conscientious student. As time passed he grew to recognize the importance of being well-trained for future service in the church. He spent more time examining pressing issues and keeping up his grades so that he could get into a seminary of his choice.

BECOMING PRESBYTERIAN

When David's pre-theological studies came to an end in the spring of 1963, David was convinced that his future laid with The Presbyterian Church in Canada. In those days a young man who desired to become a Presbyterian minister had to complete a pre-theological bachelor's degree at a recognized university (like Waterloo Lutheran) before doing a second bachelor's degree at a denominational theological seminary.

Presbyterian students in those years could study at one of two seminaries—Knox College in Toronto or The Presbyterian College in Montreal. Although at that time The Presbyterian College was

---

10. The picture was apprently printed in the *Guelph Mercury* in the Spring of 1961.

perceived by some to be more theologically conservative than Knox, this was not the reason David was drawn to it. Rather, David appreciated the College more for its smaller, more intimate setting and its proximity to French Quebec.[11] In these years the French connection at the College was considerably less than it had been in the previous century, but due to its location, contact with French-speaking people was thought more possible in Montreal than in Toronto. In any case, in September 1963 David arrived in Montreal for studies.

Although the College had been in existence for a century, it had only recently moved into its new facilities a few steps east of the campus of McGill University when David began attending.[12] The College, founded in 1865, worked together with the Methodist and Congregationalist colleges in the second decade of the 20th century but withdrew from this cooperative venture at the time of the inauguration of the United Church of Canada in 1925—a union which about a third of Presbyterian Congregations in Canada did not join.[13] Further, one of the reasons for the foundation of and growing interest in the College was the perceived overly-dominant position of Knox College in the theological life of The Presbyterian Church in Canada.[14]

David's time at the College was not only greatly beneficial, but also very challenging. On one hand, David seemed to benefit significantly

---

11. In his history of The Presbyterian College, Keith Markell notes that this proximity to French Canadians was particularly important in the college's founding. H. Keith Markell, *History of The Presbyterian College, Montreal. 1865–1986* (Montreal: The Presbyterian College, 1987), 12ff.

12. For photos of the construction see: *Presbyterian College Life* (1963): 18–19; and of the finished facilities see: *Presbyterian College Life* (1965): 14–15.

13. The United Church of Canada was founded in 1925 as a merger of four Christian denominations: two thirds of The Presbyterian Church in Canada (then the largest Canadian Protestant denomination), the Methodist Church of Canada, the Congregational Union of Ontario and Quebec, and the Association of Local Union Churches.

14. See: Markell, *History of The Presbyterian College*, 8.

from and enjoy life as a student. In his three years there David was involved in a great many student activities including the Students' Society, student retreats and attracting new students to the college.[15] He was a decent student, but was interested more in ideas and people than in academic perfection.[16]

Although he worked hard, David still loved to have fun. We can catch a glimpse of his warm-hearted personality in a short article he wrote for *Presbyterian College Life* introducing the first-year students. After kindly describing his fellow first-year students, David takes the time to let the others (tongue-in-cheek) describe him:

> Then there's me, Dave Craig, but I'm going to let the other seven do the honors. Dave comes from Guelph and is a graduate of Waterloo. Dave has done more for the female population of Montreal than the rest of us put together. From nurses, librarians, teachers, stenos to Bishops and back. Dave has blazed a trail of glory
> unequalled in the history of P.C. Don Juans. Seriously he is a
> very likable guy. Dave worked this past winter in St. Lambert and between buses tried to attend as many lectures as possible. This summer he was working for a while at home and then in June went to Labrador under the Mission Board to serve in a boomtown. His

---

15. The caption under his graduating photo in 1966 reads: "David Craig was raised in Guelph, Ontario, graduated in Arts from Waterloo University before coming to Montreal. He has been the Student assistant at St. Andrew's, St. Lambert, for his three years at P.C. David is former Vice-President of the Students' Society and during the past year has been Convener of Retreat and Recruitment. Dave and Nancy plan to enter Missionary work in the near future." *Presbyterian College Life* (1966): 7. A friendly photo of David standing with his classmates is found in *Presbyterian College Life* (1965): 20.

16. We have three sermons David presented in class: on E17 "Invitation to life" he received a 'B'; on E18 "God's Unchangeables" he received a 'B+' with the comment 'very good'; on E100 "Peculiar People" he received a 'B+'. His final transcript from Presbyterian College reveals a student who had strong marks in pastoral theology, but average ones in most other areas. Interestingly (knowing his passion for the subject), his lowest average marks came in church history!

army experience will come in handy in dealing with this exciting work.[17]

The joking aside, the fact that David was very active in seminary is true.

However, with the good times came the challenges. Many of the foundational ideas David had learned as a child and in university were now being confronted. Rather than try to tune out these challenging ideas, he sought to address them. For example, a year after David's rather comical contribution to *Presbyterian College Life*, we find a very serious call to theological purity.[18] David's article (note: by "David T. Craig" and no longer by "Dave Craig") was preceded by that of Robert Hill. Hill, a member of the graduating class, was pushing for a great deal of participation in the ecumenical movement both at the College and in Montreal in general.[19] The editors of *Presbyterian College Life* explain in a preface to David's article that the second-year student Mr. David Craig "has felt from the beginning that he, in good conscience, could not participate in the existing form of ecumenical activity. Here at the College, he has been the most fluent opponent of this type of dialogue, and as such takes the stand for the others here, who, by and large, feel as he does."[20] In the article, after giving an outline of what he considered to be "vital Christianity" David gives his view of the "current spirit of ecumenism":

> It should be obvious that denominational lines are now anachronistic. Whether speaking of Rome or of our own particular brands of Canadian Protestantism, the scandal of our own divisions is not, as we are so persistently told to believe, the mere existence of separate denominations. The real scandal which cuts across all

---

17. Dave Craig, "New Faces at P.C.," *Presbyterian College Life* (1964): 11.
18. David T. Craig, "A Dialogue about Dialogue [Part II]," *Presbyterian College Life* (1965): 10–11.
19. Robert Hill, "A Dialogue about Dialogue [Part I]," *Presbyterian College Life* (1965): 8–10.
20. *Presbyterian College Life* (1965): 8.

denominations and which is within each of them, is the absence of the "Whole Counsel of God" from our pulpits. The uncertain sound of the trumpet at the moment of battle is confusing the army. There is much evidence that many are becoming heartsick with the husks and shallow uncertainties which too many Protestants have substituted for the eternal basic truths of our Lord's Gospel.[21]

David continues the article by saying that contrary to expectations, Presbyterians ought to be more open with the new group of Catholic biblical scholars like Father de Vaux,[22] than with the "philosophizing, unbelieving, pseudo-Christian Protestant theologians" so intent on being 'ecumenical.'[23] The argument of this small article would become characteristic of David's ministry method. He would vigorously critique those who were in name close to him, but theologically very far, and encourage those who in name were very far, but theologically much closer.

This small example is indicative of a broader trend in this period of David's education. At seminary he was forced to interact with the arguments of those whom he considered 'liberal' Protestants. It is clear that he learned a great deal from his professors at the College, but some of their teaching was what he considered unedifying for "vital Christianity". For example, he cites a saying of Prof. Ritchie Bell with approval: "a minister needs to disturb the comfortable and comfort the disturbed."[24] Yet, on another occasion, he is less satisfied with one of his

---

21. Craig, "A Dialogue about Dialogue," 11.

22. Roland de Vaux was a French Dominican priest who led the Catholic team that inintially worked on the Dead Sea Scrolls. His work on ancient Israel, appearing broadly in the 1950s and 60s, was appreciated for its major contributions to the field of biblical archaeology. For a more general view of these catholic biblical scholars' influence on Canada see: John S. Moir, *A History of Biblical Studies in Canada: A Sense of Proportion* (Chico, Ca.: Scholars Press, 1982), 79–84.

23. Craig, "A Dialogue about Dialogue," 11.

24. Sermon E74. Some of his other professors would have been: C. Ritchie Bell, Donald Neil MacMillan, H. Keith Markell, Robert Lennox, Charles H.H.

professors who recommended that pastors not preach publicly on the "difficult passages" of Scripture.[25] Most of all, he frequently critiqued the thought of the 'liberal' theologians in North America and Europe (and in the Presbyterian Church) who questioned the divinity of Jesus and the authority of Scripture.[26] David suggested that he received one education in the classroom and quite another in the library of the College, a library which contained a great deal of classic Protestant texts.

Interesting is David's relationship with what he saw as 'neo-orthodox' teaching by certain professors at the College. In Canadian Presbyterianism, neo-orthodoxy had been strongly influential in the generation before David arrived at seminary, due largely to the prominent position of the Canadian Presbyterian pastor and theologian W.W. Bryden.[27] In the period after World War II many more Presbyterians had access to the European neo-orthodox theology of Karl Barth, Emil Brunner, Dietrich Bonhoeffer and Paul Tillich.[28] David often favourably quoted Barth, Brunner and especially Bonhoeffer (though not Tillich).[29] Also, he was pleased that some neo-orthodox thinkers brought Christology back into focus after years of liberal neglect. What is more, David frequently showed deep appreciation for the memorable and profound ways many of these theologians wrote about central theological problems.

This said, however, David was much more ready to admit the limits of neo-orthodox theology, especially in what he believed to be its

---

Scobie and Joseph C. McLelland.

25. Sermon 260 on Gen. 34:1–31.

26. Sermons 80, 242, 394, 500, 718, E78.

27. See: John Vissers, *The Neo-Orthodox Theology of W.W. Bryden* (Eugene, OR: Pickwick Publications, 2006).

28. John S. Moir, *Enduring Witness: A History of the Presbyterian Church in Canada* (Dawn Mills, On.: Presbyterian Church in Canada, 2004), 251.

29. For example: Sermons 38, 52, 73, 242, 280, 286, 288, 299, 305, 306, 333, 360, 514 and 727.

division between the "Bible" and the "Word of God".[30] He was alarmed that some of the more unorthodox thinkers of the neo-orthodox tradition were still challenging Christ's divinity.[31] Further, David was not impressed with what he considered to be imprecise and doctrinally vague teaching and preaching by many neo-orthodox thinkers.[32]

Although debates were not often held in class among the students, David did have many conversations outside class. In later years David recalled that he was very enamoured with his capacity to persuade others by the force of his well-developed arguments. His later reflection led him to believe that others were persuaded not so much by his stellar reasoning, but by Scripture or the manner in which the words were spoken.[33] David recounts the story of his first preaching assignment on Ephesians 6:10-12 while in seminary. He had prepared for several months, but when the time came to preach he went through his notes so fast that he was finished in less than ten minutes. Thankfully, he says, the listeners were indulgent with their young preacher.[34]

Through all this, young David was developing his own understanding of the Christian faith and the priorities for Christian ministry. Although he would study and read a great deal more in his life, he had already formed a general critique of what he considered a simplistic biblicism encountered as a child and of the theological liberalism he encountered in university and seminary. These general theological stances would be refined over time, but they were constants throughout the rest of David's life.

---

30. Years later, in his courses at the Institut Farel (now Farel Reformed Theological Seminary) on the New Testament (p.8 of course notes) and on Bibilcal Theology (p.1 passim), David critiques the Barthians for pulling the "Bible" and the "Word of God" apart.
31. Sermon 500.
32. Sermon 105.
33. Sermon 511.
34. Sermon 410.

PRACTICING PRESBYTERIANISM

David's theology was also being formed by pastoral experience. During his time at the College, David was the student assistant at St. Andrew's Presbyterian Church in St. Lambert, just south of Montreal. Serving at first under Rev. Gardiner C. Dalzell and then under Rev. Ken Barker, David got a feel for life as a pastor in this sizable suburban church. During the school year he was asked to serve about a dozen hours per week. He was to be mostly involved with youth ministry and was to preach at least once a month.[35] David greatly appreciated his time at St. Andrew's and profited from the relationships he made there. The strength of these relationships are made clear in a little thank-you letter David sent for a $25 Christmas gift he received in December 1963. David had only served the church for a few months and was extremely touched to receive this Christmas present from the elders at St. Andrew's.[36]

During the summer months, however, David took posts at several churches where he could get full-time experience. During the first summer he served in Labrador City, a boomtown that had only recently been founded to accommodate employees of the Iron Ore Company of Canada. The following summer David served in Baie-Comeau, Quebec. Like Labrador City, this city was also quite distant to the northeast of Montreal, but it gave David even more valuable pastoral experience and a chance to interact more closely with French speakers.

---

35. In a letter from C. Ritchie Bell (a professor at The Presbyterian College) to Kenneth Barker, 29 Sept. 1965, we read that for his twelve hours of work a week at St. Andrew's Presbyterian Church, David was to be paid seven monthly installments of $285. Further, prof. Bell asked Rev. Barker to write monthly reports about David's progress, his strengths and his weaknesses. [Archives of the Presbytery of Montreal at The Presbyterian College, "St. Andrew's, St. Lambert, 1965–83."]

36. David Craig, [to the elders of St. Andrew's Presbyterian Church], (28 Dec. 1963). [Archives of the Presbytery of Montreal at The Presbyterian College, "St.Andrew's, St. Lambert, 1950–64, G.C. Dalzell."]

PRESBYTERIANISM AND A KLINCK

One memory that David had of this second summer was the rickety state of his car that brought him the more than 650 kilometres to Baie-Comeau. The car, an old Pontiac, was so beat up that David had to make new sockets for the front headlights out of plastic ice cream containers. One of his congregation members was astounded that such a jalopy could make it all the way to Baie-Comeau and back to Montreal. David was unsure whether his confidence in the car was 'faith' or presumption.[37]

More significant memories about his work in Baie-Comeau are gleaned from a letter he wrote to Ken Barker back at St. Andrew's Church. In this letter David relates some of his pastoral experiences that summer.[38] First, he mentions that he is quite involved in the Young People's group. This group was special because many of these young people came from French-speaking, Roman Catholic backgrounds. In fact, one of his friends was a French Canadian who had great zeal to share Scripture with others. He and David decided to go door-to-door evangelizing the residents of Baie-Comeau. David's friend would speak in French and David would follow up with more detailed biblical exposition in English. Soon, however, they became discouraged when they realized that the Jehovah's Witnesses had already "covered the territory." David was tired of starting out every conversation by saying that he and his friend were not "Temoins Jehove." [sic] Finally, David remarks that he was learning a great deal about what it meant to minister in an area where Protestantism was definitely not in the majority.

One particular pastoral issue David encountered that summer continued to appear in his subsequent thought. While in Baie-Comeau he stayed with a family who were regular church attendees but admitted that they personally had no assurance of their salvation.[39] In fact, when

---

37. Sermon 393.

38. David Craig, Letter to Ken Barker (7 Jul. 1965). [Archives of the Presbytery of Montreal at The Presbyterian College, "St.Andrew's, St. Lambert, 1965–83."]

39. Sermons 288, 357B and E13.

David challenged them on this point, they thought he was far too proud of himself. David would use this example to point out how assurance was something which ought to be based on one's status in Christ and not on subjective feeling.

At the end of David's three years of study, he was appreciative of the pastoral experience he had received at each church. In fact, David would continue to have contact with these churches for many years. Several months after his departure in June 1966, David received a financial gift from St. Andrew's Church to support his further work. David responded with a letter thanking them for their generous gift and for all they had done for him:

> Looking back on the past three years I can really say there is no other place I would rather have been than St. Andrew's. I appreciate more than you know your warmth, trust and encouragement. I have appreciated the opportunity to learn from you all and know St. Andrew's will always hold some happy memories for me.[40]

David's deep theological links to Presbyterianism had now also become deeply personal.

A CERTAIN KLINCK

And then there was Nancy! Apart from his faith, Nancy was the constant in David's adult life.

The story actually begins much earlier than David's seminary days. In 1959 Nancy Klinck's parents went to Europe for the summer. They sent young Nancy from Quebec to Ontario to work and live with her aunt in Kitchener-Waterloo. During that summer Nancy was invited to visit Guelph Bible conference grounds where she was introduced by a mutual friend to the young David Craig. Nancy recalls that David liked the large hat she was wearing and evidently decided to get to know her

---

40. David Craig, Letter to Mr. Fay [clerk of Session at St. Andrew's Church], (9 Jun. 1966). [Archives of the Presbytery of Montreal at The Presbyterian College, "St.Andrew's, St. Lambert, 1965–83."]

better. When they met, Nancy was only 16 and she would not tell David her age until her 17th birthday. The following year Nancy went to Switzerland to study and she and David corresponded. Yet their relationship petered out. David later visited Nancy in 1961 at McGill University, but the spark was just not there (yet!).

Although Nancy was born and raised in Quebec, her family was not native to the region. Her father, William John Klinck, a medical doctor, was lured to *la belle province* by his brother-in-law Dr. Arthur Hill, also a medical doctor, to participate in the planting of a Brethren assembly. Both were actually raised in Ontario, but Arthur encouraged William to consider the importance of work in the neighbouring province. For a time Dr. Hill worked with the Presbyterian Church in Sherbrooke, but soon saw the necessity and possibility of starting a Brethren assembly in the area.[41]

Nancy, then, grew up in this mission-minded family. She was always a good student. After completing a diploma at Lennoxville High School, she studied at Neuchatel Junior College in Switzerland and earned a bachelor's degree in French from McGill. She did further training at MacDonald College and Bishop's University. She was active in sports (she was a figure skater while at McGill), and her first job was teaching French at Chambly County High School in St. Lambert, Quebec.

The romance between David and Nancy was rekindled during the 1963–64 school year when Nancy was at Bishop's University in Lennoxville for her teacher training. One day while she was visiting Montreal from Lennoxville, she and David had a chance meeting (at least Nancy recalls it as happening by chance) while crossing the street. David's interest was immediately renewed, and he began to think of how he would cross paths with Nancy again. The opportunity arose through Nancy's uncle who was also interested in David. Dr. Hill was intrigued

---

41. David and his 'Uncle Art' often wrote to each other when David returned to Quebec and began to promote the Reformed cause. His uncle encouraged him in his mission work, but was unconvinced that Reformed ecclesiology was biblically warranted or helpful in Quebec.

by David's adherence to Reformed theology and, having been a debater in university, wanted to challenge David on several points of theology. When Dr. Hill invited David to his home in Sherbrooke one weekend, David took the opportunity to invite Nancy out on a date. Unfortunately, Nancy had already booked a date with another young man that same night. David, however, was persistent and Nancy managed to see both of them in the same evening. As her first date left the back door of her house, her second date, David, was arriving at the front! This time (one imagines to the chagrin of Nancy's first, unsuspecting date) the spark was lit and David and Nancy hit it off.[42] Their lives became much closer when Nancy, like David, was assigned to a teaching post in St. Lambert just south of Montreal. This proximity allowed them to see a lot more of each other. They were engaged by February and married on 18 December 1965.[43] To remember this joyful occasion David and Nancy had their initials and wedding date—"NAK-DTC 18/12/65"—inscribed on the inside of their wedding rings.[44]

---

42. David was not only impressed with Nancy, but also with her family. David recounts with great respect that his father-in-law, a doctor, was offered a position in cancer research at The Royal Victoria Hospital in Monteral, but refused for the sake of his family, his church and his work for God. Because of his refusal to put himself first, he was able to set up an orphanage, old age homes, help in the establishment of a Brethren assembly and pay the mortgage for Bethel Bible Institute (now *Parole de Vie* in Sherbrooke). Sermon 499. On the mission work of Nancy's uncle, Dr. Arthur Hill in Quebec see also: A Donald MacLeod, *C. Stacey Woods and the Evangelical Rediscovery of the University* (Downers Grove, Il.: IVP Academic, 2007), 45, 55.

43. H.A. Welch of Grace Chapel in Sherbrooke (Nancy's home church) wrote to Ken Barker on 17 November 1965 to request that the banns of marriage be published in David's home church (which was St. Andrew's Presbyterian in St. Lambert at this time). [Archives of the Presbytery of Montreal at The Presbyterian College, "St.Andrew's, St. Lambert, 1965–83."] A very handsome picture of the couple is printed for David's graduation in the 1966 *Presbyterian College life. Presbyterian College Life* (1966): 7.

44. Nancy's middle name is Alison. Sermon 62.

Gradually, Nancy, who to this point had attended a Brethren assembly, became more convinced of the importance of Reformed theology. Although it helped that her fiancé was a future Presbyterian minister, Nancy too began to seriously consider the differences between the theology of her Brethren roots and the theology (and church structure) of the Presbyterian Church. She read with interest the letters that David was writing back and forth with her uncle in the ensuing years. In these letters David and 'Uncle Art' would discuss with love and respect the main dividing issues between the Brethren and Reformed points of view. Largely, the sticking points were baptism, an ordained clergy and, later, the wisdom of forming a new Reformed church in Quebec.[45] In any case, "Mrs. D.T. Craig" also became a member of St. Lambert Presbyterian Church on 5 June 1966, just before she and David left to begin their journey to the mission field.[46] Over the years both would continue to learn about and appreciate Presbyterianism, but at this stage they were now both officially Presbyterians.

---

45. Letters (17 Sept. 1969) and (15 Feb. 1979).

46. *St. Andrew's Presbyterian Church Newsletter* 2/7 (Sept. 1966) [Archives of the Presbytery of Montreal at The Presbyterian College, "St.Andrew's, St. Lambert, 1965–83."]

CHAPTER THREE

Missionaries!

OFF TO CALABAR

David graduated from the College[1] and was ordained at St. Andrew's Presbyterian Church in Sherbrooke, Quebec, in May 1966.[2] He chose to give a meditation on 1 Peter 5:1–4 at his ordination, pointing out that God wishes pastors to be humble servants.[3] At that time new graduates from Canadian Presbyterian Colleges were required to do service in parishes in the Canadian North or on the mission field. David and Nancy chose the latter and were sent to Nigeria.[4] Although they both had been interested in missions for

---

1. David won "The Charlotte Agnes McAllister Prize in Pastoral Theology Third Year" at his graduation, the 99th annual Convocation of the Presbyterian College, Montreal, 26 April 1966.

2. Once accepted as a missionary, the General Board of Missions directed the local presbytery to ordain David. See letter of Rodger Talbot to W.G. Clark, clerk in Presbytery of Quebec (28 Mar. 1966). [PCC Archives—File # 1990-5007-5-2.]

3. Sermon 7. In most Reformed traditions an ordinand does not preach at his own ordination, but in others two meditations are given—one by the presiding pastor and one by the ordinand.

4. In March 1966, David and Nancy wrote the General Board of Missions applying for a position in Nigeria. David and Nancy Craig, letter to GBM (15

many years, they were especially impressed by presentations given by representatives of the Board of World Missions. In particular, David noted the work of Malcolm Ransom and Earle Roberts, both of whom had influenced him as he worked at St. Lambert Presbyterian Church.[5] Ransom, the director of missionary education, and Roberts, at that time the temporary assistant to the overseas secretary, both spent a great deal of time educating young Presbyterian men and women about overseas missions.[6]

Yet, another man, E.H. Johnson, would be central to Nancy and David's work as missionaries. Johnson was the secretary for the Board of Overseas Missions in The Presbyterian Church in Canada. He was deeply interested in mission work across the globe, but especially in Nigeria. David and Nancy were two of many people sent to Nigeria under Johnson's leadership.[7] The young couple was eager to serve in conjunction with Johnson and corresponded with him at regular intervals. It was not that Johnson manipulated or overworked David and Nancy while they were there or when they came home with a story to tell, but their enthusiasm and experiences were welcomed support for Johnson's intense work in Nigeria in the 1960s. The initial appoint-

---

Mar. 1966). [PCC Archives—File # 1990–5007-5-2.]

5. This information is from an internal candidate information report of the General Board of Missions compiled in the spring of 1966. The report of two pages entitled "David and Nancy Craig" lists both David and Nancy's background, education, relationships, work experience, influences, calling, acceptance of missionary life and references. In both cases the board offered the positive assessment, "can endorse" at the end of the document. [PCC Archives—File # 103-G-3.]

6. Earle Roberts was the one charged with organizing the details of David and Nancy's trip to Nigeria. On 8 July 1966 he sent a letter to a representative of the Presbyterian Church of Nigeria to secure entry permits for David and Nancy into Nigeria. [PCC Archives—File # 103-G-3.]

7. John Alexander Johnston, "Edward Hewlett Johnson: Internationalist and Man of Peace," in: *Called to Witness: Profiles of Canadian* Presbyterians. A Supplement to Enduring Witness. Vol. 3, ed. John S. Moir (Hamilton: Committe on History, The Presbyterian Church in Canada), 99–110.

ment was for two years, but Johnson made it clear that he would have them continue if at all possible.[8]

At this time David and Nancy still knew they wanted to do mission work in a French-speaking region, but they were very happy to have the opportunity to do any sort of mission work abroad. Actually, David had already begun to better learn French (his high school French experience was not quite sufficient) and, as mentioned, took a summer preaching assignment in an area where he could interact with French-speaking people in Quebec. A friend of David's recalls that David had a desire to serve in Quebec even before he really knew how to speak the language.[9] Nancy recalls that they clearly knew they wanted to serve in a French-speaking region, but not how or when. In any case, at this juncture in their lives they were called to serve as missionaries in Calabar, Nigeria.

After a summer of mission orientation,[10] David and Nancy settled in Nigeria in the autumn of 1966. They arrived in Lagos on 3 October and made their way to Calabar in the following days.[11] In Calabar, David served as chaplain at the Hope Waddell Training Institute.[12] The

---

8. See E.H. Johnson, letter to David Craig (3 May 1966). In a letter dated 3 Mar. 1967, E.H. Johnson wrote to David, "I want to assure you that we clearly understand that your commitment is for a two year period. At the same time we would like you to be open to the leading of God and should you feel that your service in Nigeria might be extended you would find the Board at this end very responsible to planning a further tour of duty." [PCC Archives—File # 1990-5007-5-2.]

9. See: "A la mémoire de David Trevor Craig, 1937–2001," *En Lui*, special number (Mar. 2002): 9.

10. David and Nancy did several months of study at the Toronto Institute of Linguistics in Victoria Collge of the University of Toronto. See letter of Rodger Talbot to David and Nancy (9 May 1966). [PCC Archives—File # 1990-5007-5-2.]

11. Many details surrounding flights, permits and travel details can be found in the papers at The Presbyterian Church in Canada archives. [PCC Archives—File # 103-G-3 and File # 1990-5007-5-2.]

12. For more on the history of Presbyterian work in Nigeria see: Geoffrey

Institute, run officially by the Presbyterian Church of Scotland, with links to The Presbyterian Church in Canada, was a high school for boys founded in 1895.[13] It was named after Rev. Hope Waddell, a pioneering 19th century Presbyterian missionary in Nigeria, and many Presbyterian missionaries had served there over the years.[14] The Institute offered a variety of courses designed to give high quality training to students in a variety of fields.[15] Although the school had a rocky history, the 1960s were a time of relative calm.[16]

As chaplain, David interacted regularly with Hope Waddell's staff and students.[17] He lectured in Bible knowledge and a couple of days a

---

Johnston, *Of God and Maxim Guns: Presbyterianism in Nigeria, 1846–1966* (Waterloo, Ont.: Wilfred Laurier University Press, 1988), esp. 161–177; also John McNab, "Our Overseas Adventures," in: *Essays on Presbyterianism in Canada*, ed. Centennial Committee of The Presbyterian Church in Canada (Toronto: Presbyterian Publications, 1966), 107-110; Efiong U. Aye, *Old Calabar Through the Centuries* (Calabar: Hope Waddell Press, 1967); Donald M. McFarlan, *Calabar: The Church of Scotland Mission Founded 1846*. Rev. ed. (London: Thomas Nelson and Sons, 1957); Eyo Okon Akak, *A Critique of Old Calabar History* (Calabar: Ikot Offiong Welfare Association, 1981).

13. On the Hope Waddell Institute see Johnston, *Of God and Maxim Guns*, 161–177. The 'Presbyterianness' of the mission caused David to chuckle once when thinking about a church he had seen in Nigeria which was an exact replica of Presbyterian churches in Scotland. Sermon 669.

14. In sermon 649 David speaks of the history of the Presbyterian missions in Calabar: "In the cemetary of Calabar in Nigeria I saw the gravestones of about twenty young missionaries who came about a hundred years before. I saw Charles McLeod, 23 years old, Amy MacConnell, 19 years old, George Wilson, 27 years old who died of malaria because they had no medication. It was because of these young missionaries that there is a lively reformed church in Nigeria today" [translation mine].

15. Aye, *Old Calabar*, 145ff.

16. Johnston, *Of God and Maxim Guns*, 177.

17. Efiong Aye, *Old Calabar*, mentions David's coming in a note on page 149. David often talked about one of his colleagues at Hope Waddell who, although atheist, had great respect for Christians and recognized the source of Christian vitality. Sermons 432, 596 and 747.

MISSIONARIES

week he led the morning or evening chapel services.[18] David learned that a missionary had to be a jack-of-all-trades. Early on he had to settle a land dispute between a woman and one of the local chiefs.[19] He also learned of the different health risks of working in Nigeria when he contracted dengue fever and the measles in mid-November.[20]

Apart from his work at Hope Waddell, David was also a pastor responsible for fifteen congregations in the region! He realized immediately that it would be impossible to preach at all the congregations in any effective way by himself, so he trained elders from each of the local churches for the weekly charge of preaching. He would often show them how to preach and give them help with making sermon outlines.[21] When preaching himself, he would have someone standing next to him translating the sermon into the local language. Sometimes he would joke to Nancy that he felt like a "travelling priest" who gave out communion in the various churches.[22] Some of the churches he worked with were very small and out of the way, others were very large, modern churches very much like those in Scotland or Canada.[23] The work was tiring, but rewarding and very exciting.[24]

---

18. "Christmas Letter from the Craigs" (Dec. 1966).

19. Letter to parents (14 Nov. 1966).

20. At first Nancy thought David's sickness was malaria, but later found out it was dengue fever. Letter to parents (23 Nov. 1966).

21. In sermon 430 David relates that his first sermon in Nigeria was based on John 1 admonishing his hearers that 'they must be born again.'

22. Nancy relates that she and David loved to climb onto their little scooter and ride into the jungle.

23. One of the only sermons we available from David's time in Nigeria was a funeral sermon preached on two separate occasions. Sermon E43.

24. David, a Presbyterian missionary, nonetheless remembers with a bit of humour his Brethren roots: "It would do all your Brethren hearts good to see the church here in action. Everywhere we go the elders take a most active and directive role in the work of the church. At all services they sit at the front behind the communion table and have some part, either preaching, praying or leading the singing. Certainly no 'one-man' ministry here! And the church is much better off." Letter to parents (6 Dec. 1966).

In Calabar David and Nancy lived in a raised bungalow of cement blocks overlooking the Calabar River, not far from the Institute.[25] During the day, Nancy taught French at Hope Waddell to boys in their third and fourth years of study. The students did not have many of the supplies students in Canada would have had, but nonetheless were very interested in learning. In her spare time, Nancy committed herself to learning the Efik language and culture.[26] She also loved to stroll through the market with missionary friends taking in the many sights and colours.[27]

Christmas 1966 was an enjoyable time, despite being far away from their families. Nancy did her best to decorate her home without a pine tree, reindeer or snow. She asked her steward to help her hang some palm fronds (apparently the common way Nigerians decorated for Christmas) on the walls in the living and dining rooms. For Christmas Nancy bought David a game of dominoes, and he gave her a wooden hand-carved lobster and a game of chess.[28] On Christmas day David preached on the news of Christ's birth being delivered to the humble shepherds.[29] Following the service he and Nancy jumped on their Honda scooter and took a scenic drive in the country around Calabar.

In the spring of 1967 David and Nancy reported many interesting developments in their ministry. David was encouraged that in several towns new churches were being formed and evangelism committees

---

25. In a letter to her parents dated 1 Nov. 1966, Nancy gave a sketch of their bungalow complete with room descriptions, furniture placement and even plant locations.

26. Nancy's letters home to her parents and friends are tremendously fascinating with details on missionary life in Calabar during these years. Besides letters to their families, Nancy and David sent at least two official newsletters in Dec. 1966 and Mar. 1967 to their friends and supporters back in Canada.

27. "Craigs Personal Newsletter" (Mar. 1967). [PCC Archives—File # 103-G-3.]

28. Letter to parents (26 Dec. 1966). One needs to know if Nancy kept this precious Lobster . . .

29. Letter to parents (26 Dec. 1966).

were being established.[30] Hope Waddell had the privilege of showing a Moody Science film one Sunday evening. In their newsletter, David and Nancy noted that such a 'beautiful' film might be common in North America, but very unusual there. Many students were captivated by the vibrant images and creational message.[31] Nancy also became the 'patroness' of the Scripture Union club. As patroness she helped club leaders or Sunday school teachers prepare their Bible lessons.[32]

David and Nancy were very active during their time in Calabar. In a letter to their parents in February 1967, Nancy describes a 'typical' Sunday experience:

> Sometimes I really feel sorry for Dave as he is trying so hard to bring them [his congregation] a message from God. We didn't leave until 1:10. I walked home because Dave had a Session meeting after that. He arrived home at 2:15, could not find his next sermon, so in half an hour he wrote another, ate a bun, drank some juice and tore off to the next service at Big Qua Church at 3:00! I stayed at home. He will probably arrive home about 4:45 and the next service is here at H.W. [Hope Waddell] at 5:00.[33]

This rhythm continued for the next several months. The spring was hot, but full of interesting conversations and stimulating activities. Especially appreciated was the car bought by their Canadian supporters—a dark-green Peugeot 204 station wagon.[34] In their new car they went for a much needed four day vacation to the big city of Port Harcourt.[35] For

---

30. "Craigs Personal Newsletter" (Mar. 1967). [PCC Archives—File #103-G-3.]
31. "Craigs Personal Newsletter" (Mar. 1967). [PCC Archives—File #103-G-3.]
32. "Craigs Personal Newsletter" (Mar. 1967). [PCC Archives—File # 103-G-3.]
33. Letter to parents (19 Feb. 1967).
34. See Nancy Craig, letter to Laura Jackson [Secretary at GBM] (3 August 1967). [PCC Archives—File #1900-5007-5-2.]
35. Letter to parents (9 May 1967).

the summer they had wonderful plans of visiting other parts of Africa and settling down for several more years of service in Calabar.[36] They also expanded their family of animals by buying a monkey, a kitten and a genet (a cat-like animal common in Africa).[37] Unfortunately, David's work was greatly prohibited because of an accident. When driving his Honda scooter, he had to swerve out of the way of an on-coming taxi. He veered onto the sand on the side of the road, lost control and landed on his shoulder. A good Samaritan finally stopped and helped David home, after which he was taken to the hospital with a fractured clavicle. The next day, David, the optimist, was happy that he had not landed on his head or been more seriously injured. During his recuperation David and Nancy witnessed the love and community of the Nigerian church. Nancy relates:

> The Nigerians have a lovely custom of visiting people when they are ill or have had a misfortune. Our house has been seething with people for two weeks! They come in ones, twos, groups and mobs: we've had students, elders, evangelists, Ladies' Guilds and children. They arrive, some with gifts of fruit, to pray for Dave and sometimes to sing a hymn or two. One Guild had a minor service! Last Sunday I glanced thru the shutter and here was coming at least ½ of one congregation, dressed in white and slowly wending its way to our house—that was the biggest crowd! Sometimes we get a bit tired, but are so grateful for the people's thoughtfulness: some walk miles![38]

The next few weeks were difficult, but David slowly regained his strength and was once again able to keep up his normal work.[39]

---

36. Letter to parents (24 May 1967).
37. Letter to parents (31 May 1967).
38. Letter to parents (12. Apr. 1967).
39. Letter to parents (9 May 1967). See also E.H. Johnson, letter to David Craig (2 May 1967). In this letter Johnson writes that he is delighted to have news from David and Nancy and that he hopes David's collarbone will heal quickly. [PCC Archives—File # 1990-5007-5-2.]

MISSIONARIES

WAR

And then things fell apart.[40] In the spring of 1967 the south-eastern provinces of Nigeria, under General Ojukwu, attempted to secede from Nigeria as the self-proclaimed Republic of Biafra.[41] The Nigerian government under President Gowon strenuously opposed this secession and sent in the Nigerian military to suppress this uprising. Unfortunately, Calabar, the city where David and Nancy were serving, was in this new Biafran republic.

As tensions mounted David and Nancy were frequently warned by the Canadian Embassy to leave the country. But because David was not working for a Canadian governmental agency he was not forced to leave. In a letter to E.H. Johnson, David mentioned the mounting political tensions and his preparations should things get more difficult:

> Right now all Nigerians and ex-patriots are waiting anxiously to see what Ojukwu and Gowon will do next. Things seem to go on as normal, but there is the daily undertone of apprehension that reaches us via the news and word of mouth. We don't feel that we'll have to move out, but there is the possibility that imported food-

---

40. At the beginning of the letter to their parents 31 May 1967, Nancy and David wrote that "as of yesterday [30 May 1967] at 6:00 a.m., we are now living in the Republic of Biafra." They told their parents "Please don't worry. Everything is proceeding normally. If we didn't listen to the radio you'd never know anything had happened: Calabar is so far removed from everything."

41. In sermon 705 David mentions that all the subsequent African wars notably that in Rwanda, reminded him of his experiences in the war in Nigeria. For more on the Biafra struggle see: Ntieyong U. Akpan, *The Struggle for Secession, 1966-1970: A Personal Account of the Nigerian Civil War* (London: Frank Cass, 1971); Zdenek Červenka, *The Nigerian War 1967-1970* (Frankfurt am Main: Bernard & Graefe Verlag für Wehrwesen, 1971); Suzanne Cronje, *The World and Nigeria: The Diplomatic History of the Biafran War 1967-1970* (London: Sidgwick & Jackson, 1972); A.H.M. Kirk-Greene, *Crisis and Conflict in Nigeria: A Documentary Sourcebook 1966-1969* (London: Oxford University Press, 1971).

stuffs will be stopped so Dave and I and the McGraws have accumulated several kinds of canned goods in case.[42]

It was soon clear that this apprehension and preparedness were not in vain.

David felt clearly that a message of non-solidarity was being sent by every Western missionary who left a third-world country once a conflict started. David wanted to show his solidarity with the people of his region. Consequently, David and Nancy made the tough decision to split up so that David could continue his work in Calabar.[43] They were informed by the Canadian Embassy that there was one last foreign freighter, the *Isonzo*, leaving from Port Harcourt in July 1967 on which Nancy could get out—and she did.[44]

Although some people questioned David's wisdom, many viewed his decision the same way he saw it—as an act of solidarity. He wanted to be with the Nigerians in their hour of need. E.H. Johnson acknowledged the couple's solidarity in a letter dated 25 July 1967, but nonetheless allowed them to take appropriate actions if necessary:

> We are happy that you and Nancy have been able to stay put as it is terribly important to support our Nigerian friends and colleagues in these days of special trial. I am sure that your action in staying with them will earn the very deep gratitude of all who know you.

---

42. Nancy Craig, letter to E.H. Johnson (13 Apr. 1967). [PCC Archives—File # 1990-5007-5-2.] The McGraws were another missionary family serving in Calabar.

43. In one of his newsletters concerning Presbyterian missionaries around Nigeria, the Secretary for Overseas Missions of The Presbyterian Church in Canada, E.H. Johnson, noted that he had received news of the profound gratitude of the Nigerian Church for those missionaries who remained with them 'in these uncertain and difficult times.' E.H. Johnson, "Present Situation in Nigeria, October 2, 1967," PCC General Board of Missions, 2.

44. In a letter from Switzerland in July 1967 Nancy tells of her difficult journey out of Nigeria and desperate longing for news about Nigeria. Letter to Parents (25 Jul. 2967). The story of this freighter is in the *Daily Times* of Lagos (Saturday 22 Jul. 1967).

At the same time we are concerned about your safety and have discussed almost daily whether the situation called for any further action. We have concluded each time that if any action is necessary, you will take it at that end and you know that you are authorized to take whatever action seems advisable in consultation with your Scottish and Nigerian colleagues. I hope it may be possible for you to continue to serve with them. May God guide you as to what actions you should take if a moment of decision comes in regard to remaining or leaving.[45]

Indeed, by the time this letter reached David, Nancy was already gone. David, however, was more convinced than ever that he wished to be present and to help in whatever way possible.[46]

Difficulties came when the Nigerian government launched a "police action" to retake the secessionist territory. The war began on 6 July 1967 and continued for several years of advances, repulsions, siege and stalemate. During this time David continued to labour. Since the school was closed, he had to find other meaningful work to fill his time.[47] He took on the responsibility of serving as letter carrier for other missionaries between his region and neighbouring Cameroon.[48] This route was extremely dangerous; there were often roadblocks and militia members, but he found this work to be quite thrilling. In September Nancy passed on news of David's clandestine work to the mission's board:

---

45. E.H. Johnson, letter to David Craig (25 Jul. 1967). [PCC Archives—Box # 1990-5007-5-2.]

46. In September 1967, E.H. Johnson wrote to David: "I do not need to tell you that you and our other friends in Nigeria have been continuously in our thoughts and prayers during these past weeks and months. It is good that some of our Canadian people have continued with the church in Nigeria so as to support it by fellowship and work. I know that your own service will be of very great value at this time of need." (5 Sept. 1967). [PCC Archives—File 1990-5007-5-2.]

47. David, letter to Nancy (1 Aug. 1967).

48. David felt that the Nigerian church and its work was the only pre-war institution that survived throughout the war. Sermon 447.

Yesterday (written Sept. 1) I received a second letter from Dave via this new address in the Camerouns. Needless to say I was thrilled! Let me quote you what he says: 'We are running a smuggling route for mail and missionaries down the Mamfe road. I am in charge... The latest news is that Gowon has Russian jets. There are the occasional rumours of bombing but the tension, especially in Calabar is much less.'[49]

Finally, in October 1967 the Nigerian government forces attacked the town of Calabar.[50] The subsequent several weeks were some of the most intense and thrilling moments in David's life.

---

49. Nancy Craig, letter to Rodger Talbot (8 Sept. 1967). [PCC Archives—File # 103-G-3.] On the Russian involvement in the war see: Cronje, *The World and Nigeria*, 252–280.

50. Intensely propagandic literature was produced by the Nigerian Federal government for the first official visit to Calabar of the military governor after its 'liberation'. *The Maiden Visit of Governor Esuene: An Account of the first official visit of His Excellency Colonel U.J. Esuene, Military Governor of South-Eastern State, to Calabar after the liberation of the town* ([No Place]: Department of Information, South Eastern State of Nigeria, Calabar; Ministry of Home Affairs and Information, 1968).

CHAPTER FOUR

The Longest Moment of David Craig

It changed him, he says, and if what he believed needed testing, it was tested then, facing the Nigerian rifles.[1]

ERNEST HILLEN

Weekend Magazine 18/4 (27 Jan. 1968) pp. 2–7.[2]

[3] ONE NIGHT a few months ago, David Craig, aged 28, was sitting tightly roped to a small steel chair, half-naked, in the depths of Africa. The air was hot and humid and mosquitoes were swarming around

---

1. In a news release sent around to Presbyterian churches and church leaders dated 24 January 1966, the General Board of Missions highly recommended this article: "This [article] is a break-through for Missions to be featured in the secular press and we commend it to your attention ... It is worth buying a copy and telling your friends about it. It might even be a good idea to have some extra copies on hand to share with church people or other friends." [PCC Archives—File # 103-G-3.]

2. This article is reproduced here with kind permission of *The Gazette*. Originally the *Weekend Magazine* was a supplement to the *Montreal Star*. After folding in 1979, the *Star*'s building and presses were acquired by *The Gazette*. I have also received permission and encouragement from the article's author, Ernest Hillen. I have added the page numbers of the original in square brackets throughout the article.

him. He was exhausted, hungry and he had to go to the bathroom. He had been shoved, pushed, slapped and humiliated. He was the victim of a ludicrous case of mistaken identity, but the band of armed men holding him didn't know this—and they wanted to kill him.

David Craig was born and raised in Guelph, Ont., graduated from Presbyterian College, McGill University, Montreal, in May 1966, and has been married for almost two years. During his college days he spent three summers serving in the Canadian army. He is six feet tall, has a pale face and wears horn-rimmed glasses. He is a gentle man. He also doesn't talk easily about his personal feelings.

He sat through that night alone; quite alone, except when some of the men came to taunt and threaten him. But David says he was not alone.

A few hours before, with his back to that of another man, he had sat on the ground facing certain death. David says this is an experience that is never forgotten. It colors the life you live after it; it affects the decisions you make, the values you cultivate. It changes you. And if anything you believe in was in need of testing, it will have been tested then.

This is what happened:

About 18 months ago David was ordained a minister of The Presbyterian Church in Canada and shortly afterwards sent out to serve as missionary for two years in Nigeria. He and his wife, Nancy, who is 25 and from Lennoxville, Que., were located in the port city of Calabar in the eastern region of the country, about 130 miles from the border of the Cameroon Republic. On May 30 last year, Lt.-Col. Odwumegwo Ojukwu declared the region the independent Republic of Biafra, and ever since there has been fierce fighting between his forces and those of the Nigerian federal government.

It is a confusing war which, to some extent, is also a tribal conflict. The Ibos, one of the largest of Nigeria's more than 50 distinctive tribes, form the majority in Biafra, and they are an intelligent, ambitious and forceful people.

THE LONGEST MOMENT OF DAVID CRAIG

One feature of it, as of all African wars today, is the mercenary, the professional soldier who hires himself out to whoever pays most. There is pressure on the men of both sides to catch these killers. They have immense propaganda value if the world press can be shown that the other side has to employ them. Mercenaries are dangerous fighters and some black soldiers fear them, believing they, have 'Juju' or special magic power.

David and Nancy Craig almost immediately liked living in Calabar. The people (the Efik tribe lives in the area) were friendly and hospitable, many of them spoke English, and most were Christian.

David had been appointed chaplain of the Hope Waddell Training Institution in Calabar and taught 'Bible' there. He also served as pastor to six churches in the city and nine in the bush. Nancy, beside her household duties, taught French at the Institute and applied herself to the Efik language. One thing both say they discovered quickly: they were learning a lot more from the Efiks than they were teaching them.

It was a good life. The Craigs were liked. How much, they found out after David had an accident and broke his collarbone. Visitors started coming in droves the very next day, from as far away as 10 jungle miles, on foot, to see the sick 'Etubom' (meaning 'master of the canoe' and a highly complimentary term) and wish him good health. Nancy counted that in the few weeks David was laid up they entertained more than 500 visitors.

In July the war had grown so serious all foreigners were urged to leave the area. Even Biafrans who had married white women sent their wives away. Nancy left on the last evacuation ship for Lagos. From there she flew to Switzerland, stayed a few weeks waiting for the situation to calm down, but when it didn't returned home to Lennoxville. Only the occasional letter came from David and then it might be six weeks old. To ease the waiting she got a job as a hostess at Expo.

The fighting between Nigerian and Biafran troops grew more intense. Foreign businessmen and government people had left the Calabar area long ago and, by now, so had most missionaries. In the end David remained the only white man within a radius of 50 miles in a vicious war between black men.

"I wanted to stay with these people," he says. "I knew there wasn't much I could do, but I felt that just being there, being seen going about my normal work, perhaps might do something . . ."

The Nigerian navy now brought ships into the battle. (Ironically, at Nigeria's national day celebrations at Expo on Oct. 12, Nancy shook hands with Rear Admiral Joseph Abet Wey, commander of the Nigerian navy. Orders for the naval attack on Calabar must already have been under way.)

"It was Wednesday, Oct. 18, 6 A.M.," David recalls in his precise way, "when I awoke in our house on the grounds of the Institute to hear what sounded like thunder. It came from down river from the vicinity of the town of Oron. At first I didn't think anything of it. Oron had been lightly shelled before. But the gun fire continued and seemed to be coming closer. Two hours later I glanced out the window toward the river, heard a muffled boom, and saw a large water spout rise a half mile from shore. I recall thinking, 'Thank God, Nancy has gone.' The firing went on, getting closer and closer."

A few minutes later, a missionary colleague drove [4] up in a Land Rover and asked if they shouldn't pick up two missionary women and their children and get them to safety across the Cameroon Republic border.

While the colleague started loading the women's luggage which was at the school, David drove out to pick them up at their quarters in the centre of town. He had passed the Calabar Club when 100 yards ahead there was a terrific blast. A shell from the four-inch naval guns had landed. He moved on when the smoke cleared, but further up Biafran troops had sealed off the road. He turned around to try and circle Calabar and enter it from the other side. Hordes of panicked refugees, many running in opposite directions, clogged the way.

"Little black clouds of shell bursts scattered over the city. Women screamed, children cried. I had to stop often to avoid hitting people. When I got to the other road Biafran troops had sealed it off, too. On the way back I picked up Mrs. Iso, a member of one of my congregations, her daughter and grandchildren. They were running and hysterical. I wanted to pick up more people but the car was packed."

He drove Mrs. Iso to a plantation four miles out of Calabar. There he learned that his colleague had been seen with the missionary women and their children heading for the Cameroon border. Via a small place called Big Qua Town, David drove back to the school. Everything seemed quiet, deserted.

"I opened the car door, put one foot on the ground, and then the air seemed to, explode. Almost overhead naval shells were bursting in the trees. I hit the ground, and machine gun fire went over the roof of the car. Then there was a lull I got up and ran. Fire opened up and down I went. Another lull and I'd get up and run till the next burst."

He made it to the rear of the school and dove into a shallow trench. Just in time, machine-gun fire skimmed over the edge of the trench and hit into the trees behind. Naval guns seemed to be moving closer too. Then something bit him, and again and again. He was lying on top of a nest of black ants, and he was wearing short pants. For several minutes he couldn't move as the bullets were still flying overhead. During the next lull, he scrambled out of the trench, left the school grounds and made his way back to Big Qua Town to the house of a friend, a church elder.

The house of Okokon Bassey was big, with thick concrete walls. There were others who had sought refuge there, most of them children, and there was a young woman with a new-born baby. Evening came and with it mosquitoes. Bassey loaned David a native wrap-around to protect his legs.

During the night the battle raged on. Mortar fire became heavy and the house next door was hit.

Early next morning, still wearing the wrap-around, David took a cautious look outside. Nigerian forces now seemed to have the upper hand. They had set up checkpoints at both ends of the street. He got quite close to one of them without being seen and then witnessed what he calls "one of the horrors of war."

"A group of Efik people brought two young men in civilian clothes to the soldiers. The lads looked like high school students. One soldier spoke Efik and he questioned the prisoners in it to see if they spoke with an Ibo accent. Apparently they did. Without further ado the soldiers took aim, fired, and the two young men fell down dead in the street."

David turned away, sickened, and walked back to the house. He later heard eye witness accounts of similar atrocities by the Biafran forces.

He had noticed the Basseys had almost no food and now he proposed that he and Bassey should go to one of the checkpoints and ask if they might fetch some for the family from David's house. Bassey agreed.

On approaching the checkpoint they were ordered to put up their hands. The officer in charge, a young 2nd lieutenant, took a hard, long look at David, spat on the ground, then told two of his men to take him around to the back of the nearest house. There they stood him up against the wall, arms high, facing them. Never once did their fingers leave the triggers of their rifles.

"You are a Chinese mercenary!" one of them suddenly shouted. "You have been paid by Ojukwu."

It's unlikely they ever saw a Chinese, says David, but for political reasons the soldiers may have been encouraged to dub all mercenaries Chinese.

David told them quietly, that he was from Canada. He said that he was a missionary, not a mercenary. But the two words have an unfortunate similarity.

"Take off your glasses," ordered the same soldier. David took them off and put them in a pocket. "If you are a missionary—prove it. Where is your collar?"

Clerical collars are uncomfortable in the tropics and David wore his as rarely as he could.

For a very long moment the soldier stood looking at David, clearly undecided whether to shoot him or not. Then he grabbed him, swung him around and pushed him forward.

"I'm taking you to the colonel," he said.

THE LONGEST MOMENT OF DAVID CRAIG

Bassey was collected from the checkpoint, and with the soldiers prodding from behind with their rifles he and David were marched off the street onto a bush path.

"I half expected to be shot then and there," David recalls. "The path was out of sight and deserted."

They stopped at the entrance to the courtyard of a large cement factory. The white-washed gate was smeared with blood. So were some of the outside walls of the factory, David saw later.

Apparently the factory had been taken over as temporary army quarters. Groups of soldiers pressed toward the two prisoners when they came in. The men were armed and in sweat-soaked battle dress. Bassey was almost ignored; it was David they wanted a closer look at. Here, finally, was one of the deadly specimens—a live mercenary—and he was in their power.

One, ripped off his shirt, spinning him around with the force of it. Another yanked his watch from his wrist. A third put his face a half-inch from David's and spat. An NCO ordered his shoes cut off, and a knife slit through the laces so he could shake them loose.

It happened then. Somebody pointed to David's wrap-around. Among the various designs, quite by coincidence, was one of a rising sun—the symbol of Ojukwu's forces.

This started an uproar. Here was positive proof he was a mercenary—and mercenaries must die. There were cries of "Let me do it! Let me! Let me shoot him!" Loud arguments arose as to who should have the privilege. But the NCO cut this short with an order to the effect that they all would.

David recalls that up to then everything had happened so rapidly he had just accepted events as they came. There had been something dreamlike about it. But now it was a dream no longer.

The two prisoners were pushed further into the yard and then told to sit down, back to back.

"One soldier gave me a heavy blow on the side of [6] the head. I found it difficult to hear for a couple of minutes. Then the NCO shouted:

"'Take your positions!'

"The soldiers formed a wide circle around us. I heard the NCO say to one of them:

"'Move back. You know what happens when a bullet hits the ground.'

"Another soldier suddenly walked up to me and pointing at my wedding ring, demanded: 'What is that?' He probably thought it some kind of Juju protection.

"'Take it off!'

"I did, and he grabbed it and heaved it away. I thought, 'Can't they even leave me that . . .'[3]

"Someone shouted: 'If you are not a mercenary why did you stay when you were told to get out?'

"I replied in as loud a voice as I could muster: 'Because God asked me to stay with His people in their trouble.'

"'You'll stay all right!' another voice called out.

"I didn't hear the order but the soldiers now began cocking their weapons and I heard safety catches clicking off.

"'May God forgive you!' I called out, and then I bowed my head to pray.

"'Lift up your head! Open your eyes!' they yelled. The rifles were pointing at us. They were taking aim."

What was he thinking? Was he afraid of the men standing there with their rifles? Did he hate them?

"The rifles were very real—FN–C1s. I knew them well from my army days. I knew their power, their precision. I was aware of the hatred and loathing in the men's faces. But I didn't feel it for them . . . it was all such a hideous error. I was aware of [7] the hot air and of the blood-smeared

---

3. [In his letter to Nancy of 5 Nov. 1967, David writes "My darling the very lowest point I reached was when they threw away a part of you—my wedding ring. But don't worry dear, I have it back. Someone (kinder than the rest) looked for it and returned it to me.]

walls. I was very aware of everything . . . of the clearness of my own mind. I thought with surprise, 'I'm thinking so clearly.'

"I wasn't afraid in my *mind*. My body probably was afraid; had been afraid all along perhaps. You see, I never once felt I was really alone. Of this I was quite certain—God was with me.

"I thought of Nancy, of course. The image of her was very real . . . "

"Stop!" yelled a voice. It was the batman of the commanding officer. "The colonel wants to see him."

The soldiers were not pleased, but they obeyed the order and the guns were lowered reluctantly. As for David . . . his feeling of relief can be left to the reader's imagination. David recalls saying this to himself, almost laconically:

"Well, I guess God has more work for me to do."

He and Bassey were separated; he learned later Bassey was soon released. He had probably gotten into the mess only because he was with David.

David was taken to see Col. Echefu, who questioned him closely about his work and about Biafran troop movement and positions. He seemed to doubt David's story but tentatively agreed that the next day David would be escorted to his house to fetch his passport and papers to identify himself.

Then he ordered David returned to the court yard and bound to a chair and a two-man guard set.

Night fell. One of the guards was particularly surly. Every once in a while he told David he may have escaped that afternoon, but that he would definitely be shot next morning.

Other soldiers drifted up to have a look at the "Chinese mercenary." They too assured David he would die the next day. This happened about 25 times. They would thump their chest with an open hand and say, "Tomorrow—you get it!"

"I wondered," says David, "if they weren't planning to shoot me during the night. They could simply say that I tried to escape."

He asked the guards if he could go to the bathroom. No. They had no permission to let him.

At some time during the early part of the night the CO's batman came by and, without a word, gave him a bit of rice to eat.

It was impossible to sleep sitting upright tied to the small steel chair. The mosquitoes had a field day on his nakedness. The collarbone, only recently healed, hurt from the strain of his bound arms. In the distance, firing and mortar shelling continued.

Next morning his hands and feet were very swollen. Towards noon he was untied, given coffee and biscuits and finally allowed to go to the bathroom. Then he was taken to the colonel.

"Mr. Craig," the colonel said, "I don't think you are the mercenary we are looking for. But why did you stay?"

He had been asked that before, David said, and no one seemed to understand. What would the colonel think if a missionary came to his, the colonel's village and then decide to leave his people in their time of trouble?

After a pause, the colonel said, "I see your point."

An escort took David to his house. When he returned to the cement factory there was a delegation of local people headed by a Ntoe (paramount chief) appealing on his behalf to Col. Echefu, identifying him as their minister.

This and the papers convinced the colonel.

"You are a very lucky man, Mr. Craig," he said. "My men could easily have shot you and said they found you behind a machine gun."

The CO's batman gave him his glasses back, which had been in the shirt ripped off the day before, his wedding ring and his watch.

Later, the soldier who first had David up against a wall came over and said, "You must be a man of God. He protected you. I almost pulled that trigger."

David agrees: "I was never once alone."

There were other incidents before he reached the safety of Lagos a few days later. He was shot at repeatedly, and the ship that took him to the nation's capital was loaded with ammunition and petrol. It was bombed and shelled but never hit. But this was almost anti-climactic after his "longest moment."

In Lagos the Canadian High Commissioner thought it best that he go home till the situation improved a bit.

David and Nancy Craig want to return to Calabar as soon as possible. It may be just a matter of weeks before they do. David will finish out his second year of duty, and then he plans to sign up for another two to three years.

The Etubom should get quite a reception from his people—the story of his adventures is well known there now.

CHAPTER FIVE

Alive!

A PRESUMED DEATH

The war had disastrous consequences for the people in the secessionist territories. Besides the many dead and wounded, numerous suffered from starvation or sickness. This conflict was one of the first African wars to receive intense international aid and media attention, with images of the dead and dying regularly making headlines around the world.[1] How could one man live through such carnage and misery?

Needless to say, Nancy was very worried about David during this time. This was a time when even a simple telephone call was difficult to make from this part of Africa. Apart from letters that took several weeks to arrive in North America, David had no easy way to tell Nancy the turbulent news from the mission field. Nancy was working that summer as the head hostess at the dynamic 'Sermons from Science'

---

1. Červenka, *The Nigerian War*, 153-164; Thierry Hentsch, *Face au Blocus: La Croix-Rouge internationale dans le Nigéria en guerre (1967–1970)* (Geneva: Institut Universitaire de hautes études inernationales, 1973); Cronje, *The World and Nigeria*, 210–224.

pavilion at *Expo 67*.[2] One day she heard that there was a special Nigeria day at *Expo* and, having had intimate contact with the country earlier in the year, went to meet the Nigerian delegation.[3] One of the important persons in the delegation was the same Nigerian admiral who was at that very time, one would presume, setting up the attack on the city where David was residing. In any case, she soon heard this news herself, that a major offensive had been made against the area in which David was ministering, and she feared greatly for his life.

One day her brother Stephen, who at the time was working at the pulp and paper exhibition at *Expo 67*, received a news update in his pavilion that he brought directly to Nancy: Calabar had been attacked by ten thousand government troops! Because Nancy did not know the real story, the newsflash had a clear implication—her beloved husband was dead.

---

2. On the significance of this pavilion and *Expo 67* more generally see: Richard Lougheed, Wesley Peach and Glenn Smith, eds. *Histoire du Protestantisme au Québec depuis 1960: Une Analyse Anthropologique, Culturelle et Historique* (Quebec: La Clarière, 1999), 10, 84–86; Joseph C. McLelland, *Understanding the Faith: Essays in Philosophical Theology*. Presbyterian College Studies in Theology and Ministry, Vol.1 (Toronto: Clements Academic, 2007), 180–182.

3. The government of Nigeria published special reports on Nigeria handed out at the Nigeria Pavilion at Expo 67: *Federal Nigeria*. XI.13 (Aug. 1967). The publication is very clear in outlining the Federal government's position vis-à-vis Lt.-Col. Ojukwu. "The Head of the Federal Military Government regrets that some innocent Nigerians in the three Eastern States will suffer considerable hardship and possible loss of lives in the difficult days ahead through the blind and inordinate political ambition of Lt.-Col. Ojukwu . . . The Federal Military Government has warned all countries and international organisations to respect the territorial integrity of the Federal Republic of Nigeria. He has also appealed to them to avoid giving any support whatsoever to Ojukwu's rebel group," 24. On the Nigerian pavilion see pages 39–41.

ALIVE

COMING HOME

Thankfully the newsflash, and its implication, were not accurate. First, the size of the Nigerian force was about one thousand men and not ten thousand. Second, David was now safely in Lagos. True, he had had many near-death experiences, but he was still in the land of the living!

The story could not be kept secret. Somehow a Canadian reporter heard David was in Lagos and arrived to interview him. David agreed to tell his story on the condition that the reporter not print it in the Canadian press until he had a chance to contact Nancy. The reporter did not hold up his end of the bargain. Rather, one night Nancy received an excited phone call telling her to turn on her television immediately—David was on the news! By the time she got to a television the story had already passed, but when she called the television station she learned that the day's newspaper was also carrying the story on the front page. She ran down to a local variety store to buy a newspaper and see for herself that David was alive. Alive!

It probably felt like an eternity, but David finally contacted Nancy and told her all about his many harrowing adventures. In a long letter he wrote to Nancy in detail all that had happened to him. Nancy was overjoyed! In speaking to each other, they agreed that David would try to find a missionary post in Lagos and that Nancy could come soon to meet him there.

Consequently, David also contacted the General Board of Missions to learn of new possibilities for service. On 24 October he sent a telegram to the Presbyterian Church offices in Toronto with the cryptic phrase, "GREETINGS FROM LAGOS NARROW ESCAPE SAFE LETTER FOLLOWS AWAITING INSTRUCTIONS."[4] Although he had escaped Calabar, there were still lingering rumours about his being a mercenary. Hence, the Board of Mission, encouraged by Canadian

---

4. The original telegram is in The Presbyterian Church in Canada Archives—File # 103-G-3.

embassy officials, counselled him to leave Nigeria for the moment so as to not exacerbate the situation.

Getting out of the country would prove to be a final adventure. David accompanied Ross Hall, the minister of Lagos Presbyterian Church, on his trip home. When they arrived at the airport, they noticed that checkpoints were set up to screen those departing so as to not let out those responsible for encouraging Biafran separation. David was quite sure that his name would still be on such a list—he feared he would be imprisoned again. Yet when David and Rev. Hall arrived at the wicket, the officer could not verify his name for he had momentarily misplaced the list. The officer saw that Rev. Hall was wearing his clerical collar and asked if David was with him. When Rev. Hall vouched for David, the officer let them through with a wave and went back to his search for the list. David was happy to be going home.

Nancy had not yet heard that David was on his way home. After the close of *Expo 67* at the end of October, she returned to stay with her parents in Sherbrooke awaiting news from David. One night in early November she was invited to speak about her missionary experience in Nigeria before a women's guild meeting at St. Andrew's Presbyterian Church in Sherbrooke. One of the ladies kindly asked her: "when do you hope to see David again?" She replied that she really had no idea. At the end of the evening she returned home heavy-hearted only to be met by her father at the back door. With an unforgettably joyful look on his face, he told Nancy to go immediately to her room because this would be one of the greatest days of her life. There dozing in her bed, thin as a rail, but alive and well, was David.[5]

---

5. David tells the story in much the same way: "After having been a prisoner of war in Nigera and finally being freed, I was able to come back to Montreal. I had not seen Nancy in more than four months! I arrived at Dorval without anyone knowing. I came to my parents-in-law hungry and tired. My father-in-law held me tight and told me: 'David, go lie down up stairs—Nancy will wake you when she comes!' Two hours later, Nancy arrived and her father said to her: 'go upstairs—there is a surprise in your room!' Nancy came up to

David's family was also relieved that he was alive and back in Canada. His siblings were excited to see their brother make headlines in the news across the country, and were relieved that the headlines were that David's life was spared, not lost. He and Nancy made a trip to Ontario to recount the story to his family in person. His mother was particularly proud of her son—she showed great emotion when hearing his harrowing tale and thanked the Lord for sparing his life. David's father was full of praise to the Lord for David's safe-keeping and all that David had accomplished.

---

find someone sleeping in her bed. She turned on the lights and, what a surprise! What a reunion! Unforgettable!" Sermon 205 [translation mine].

CHAPTER SIX

A Story to Tell

MISSIONARY EDUCATION

David's story was seen by the Mission Education Committee of The Presbyterian Church in Canada as a prime way to excite the youth to consider a missionary calling and the old to give financial support. Just one year earlier the Mission Education Committee had drawn up "Deputation Guidelines" for just such an occasion. In these guidelines it was made clear that deputation is "carefully planned visiting of churches by Home or Overseas missionaries for the purpose of education in mission."[1] The care in planning was not to be understated: "Deputation may be a part of a tour of Presbytery or Synod or it may be a single visit to one congregation. Whichever, it must be carefully planned and every opportunity used to take full advantage of the wide range of experience and the new insights that such a visiting missionary brings."[2] Further, the deputation tour was to be well-publicized, for it was not to promote antiquated models of

---

1. "Deputation Guidelines" (24 Feb. 1967): 1. [PCC Archives—File # 1988-1003-80-5.]

2. "Deputation Guidelines" (24 Feb. 1967): 1. [PCC Archives—File # 1988-1003-80-5.]

missions, but "modern missions." For this reason the report stipulated, "complete, well-planned publicity prior to the missionary's arrival is essential. It is important to bear in mind that the common caricature of the missionary has to be overcome in the minds of many people and advance publicity should make clear that this is modern missions that is being discussed."[3]

Malcolm Ransom, director of the Mission Education Committee, personally corresponded with a pastor, making the purpose of David's deputation clear. The goal was not simply to have large crowds, but for David and Nancy to have "significant visits" within the various communities. He explained:

> By 'significant visit' I mean one which is planned carefully, ahead of time and for which the congregation and the community at large is well prepared; one that does not just include formal church services but which provides a maximum number of informal contacts with individuals and small groups; one that will make sure that he gets an opportunity to meet with your Session and Board of Managers; and, since David is young and has an exciting and challenging story to tell, one that will make a real effort to get him into contact with young people. Such a visit should also take into account the possibility of David addressing schools as he is well equipped to do on the timely topic of Nigeria and should try to reach other non church groups or other denominations in the community. For the details of such a visit I refer you to the relevant sections of 'Deputation Guidelines' which I enclose a copy.[4]

Further, Ransom notes the value of David's contribution to the cause of Presbyterian missions: "Mr. Craig is in such demand that we feel we can make him available only where we get the assurance that he will be

---

3. "Deputation Guidelines" (24 Feb. 1967): 1. [PCC Archives—File # 1988-1003-80-5.]

4. Malcolm Ransom, letter to Rev. William Black (4 Jan. 1968). [PCC Archives—File # 1988-1003-80-1.]

used to the maximum possible advantage. I am sure you will find too that such a planned weekend will be most satisfying and rewarding."[5]

True to these new guidelines, David and Nancy's tour of Canada was the model of modern deputation. Their deputation report papers show almost constant travel and presentations during these several months.[6] Hundreds of letters and phone calls were made to coordinate their speaking engagements. Although Ransom oversaw the voyage, his assistant, Ms. Mavis Kirk, wrote the many letters needed to put everything in place. It was no mean task! Records reveal that David and Nancy's deputation tour involved hundreds of people. Interestingly, most of these people were quite enthusiastic in their interest in having David and Nancy speak in their region.[7] Most considered it an honour to take part in such a speaking tour.[8]

David and Nancy told their story in many different settings and to varied audiences. They shared their amazing near-death missionary story with community groups, churches and also on radio and television.[9] Posters and mini-biography pamphlets were sent out to each

---

5. Malcolm Ransom, letter to Rev. William Black (4 Jan. 1968). [PCC Archives—File # 1988-1003-80-1.]

6. See their missionary deputation report [PCC Archives—File # 1988-1003-80-1.]

7. For example, see a newsletter edited by A. Summer of Labrador City called *Carol News* 3/44 (29 Aug. 1968). This newsletter was not produced by the Board of World Missions and although homemade, it nonetheless gave an interesting report on David and Nancy's missionary work and their visit to Labrador City. Hence, although it was not produced by the Board of World Mission it captured perfectly the missionary spirit with which it sent David and Nancy out. [PCC Archives—File # 1990-5007-5-2.]

8. For all this correspondence see [PCC Archives—File # 1988-1003-80-1.]

9. David was interviewed many times in newspapers, on the radio and even on television: "Un missionnaire canadien a failli être fusillé comme mercenaire," *La Presse* (Tuesday, 31 Oct. 1967): 44; Interview by Bill McNeill on CBC Radio's "Assignment" on 7 Oct. 1968; Interview by Don Sims on CBC television's (CBLT) "Luncheon Date" on 23 Jan. 1968. With sermon E64 is

community announcing their arrival. Sometimes the groups were small, but often large gatherings were present to hear them.

Although regularly quite drained, they were still encouraged when people stayed to talk with them for hours after the official presentation had ended. David and Nancy wrote to their friends that they were presenting to twelve meetings per week on average with little sleep. Yet they wanted their friends to pray for them so that they could "present Christ and the challenge of missions, not our personalities. Please share with us this, that God will empty us of ourselves and speak through us."[10]

While the travel schedule was not enviable and they were tired by the end, both David and Nancy had a continuously strong desire to educate others about what was happening in the church and society in Nigeria. Further, David's experiences were integral in his desire to serve the Lord. Evidence of this is seen in his sermons. In fact, besides the stories of the Reformation, to which we will return, no other adventure in David's life provided as much material by which to introduce biblical truth. Above all he recounted his escape from the firing squad as an example of God's grace.[11] He often told how one of his friends interceded for him in front of the colonel. This man risked his life so that David could live. Obviously, the parallels with Christ's gift for us were clear for David.[12]

---

a bulletin with a handsome photo of David and Nancy used on their cross-country travels in 1968. Under the photo is a short biography of David and Nancy's missionary adventures in Nigeria. David thinks missiologically about Nigeria in sermon E80. In E85 David mentions that he needed God's help for confidence during these many radio and TV interviews.

10. Newsletter to friends (3 Apr. 1968). [PCC Archives—File # 103-G-3.]

11. Sermon 479; David recounts in sermon 681 that being spared in Nigeria was one of the three greatest 'miracles' of his life (his adopted children and the constant financial care of God being the other two); in sermon 413 David recounts that he had never suffered such great physical hunger than at this point in his life.

12. Sermons 137, 633, 685, 772, E63; in sermon E77 David mentions that

While David frequently referenced his escape from the firing squad, he also had many other profound experiences while in Nigeria. For example, he was saddened by the spiritual poverty of other religions in Nigeria. Often he would point out that these other religions had Christian-sounding rituals, but used them for futile ends.[13] Contrasted with these religions was the simple beauty of the Christian faith. David was greatly humbled by the humility and generosity of the Christians in Nigeria.[14] Further, in many of his sermons David mentioned many

---

God saved his life at least 23 times in these several days.

13. Sermons 266, 274, 435; Sermon 309 talks of his night guard who spoke of Allah's will at the end of each phrase, but knew nothing of God's real will; Sermon 326 speaks of various bizarre and harmful forms of government in the tribes of southern Nigeria; Sermon 358 speaks of a terrible sickness caused by starvation which was common in his area of Nigeria; Sermon 571 speaks of a medical missionary who was working for real change in Nigerian life; Sermon 621; Sermon 679 speaks of how Christians were viewed as 'courageous' by non-Christians in Nigeria because they would go out of their houses at night when evil spirits were thought to roam about; Sermon E52 is a short summary and critique of animist doctrine and practice; In sermons 323 and E68 David recounts how a medical missionary of the Presbyterian church took them to a lengthy animist ceremony in the forest where a young couple brought a rooster to be sacrificed to implore the spirits to give them a baby. David was very interested in the symbolism of 'propitiation', but notes that this propitiation, in contrast to that of Christ on the cross, is unable to do anything (see also letter to parents 28 Mar. 1967 for more on this incident); In E87 David relates that when he first arrived in Nigeria he was shocked by the number of people who believed that sickness was their own fault; In sermon 339 David relates that at one Christian funeral in Nigeria several non-Christians gave hopeless wails when the body was buried. David said that he would never forget the words of one of the elders present who told these non-believers to stop wailing because the deceased person was a Christian and would rise again. Rather than wailing, said the elder, they should also believe in God.

14. Sermon 189 tells of a model of the Nigerian model of *koinonia*—true Christian community; Sermon 230 tells of the Bassey family and the love that Mr. and Mrs. Bassey had for one another; Sermons 231 and E82 tells of the joy an elderly Nigerian woman had despite her many and difficult periods of suffering; Sermon 235 speaks of personal responsibility in difficult situations

cultural differences between Western society and Nigeria.[15] He also contrasted the vitality of the Reformed Church in Nigeria with the continuing loss of public presence and vitality by the Protestants in the West.[16]

---

in the context of Nigeria; Sermon 486 speaks of the liturgical dancing in the Nigerian churches which meshed well with singing and prayer; Sermon 602 speaks of the beautiful dying words of a Nigerian man who said, 'I'm coming Lord, I'm coming'; Sermon 637 he mentions the mission in Calabar; Sermon E12 mentions the many sacrifices by Christians in Nigeria; In sermon E55A David recalls that an elderly Nigerian once told him: 'I always knew there was a God, but when I met Jesus, at last God had a face'.

15. Sermon 238 mentions that a closed door in Nigeria was a sign of exclusion; Sermons 284 and E16 mention that a Nigerian normally connects his well-being to the well-being of others—interdependence; In sermon 358 David recounts how as a prison chaplain he once saw a prisoner with a look of great joy. This prisoner had had a new trial and was now declared innocent. He was so joyful because in the morning he would be released from prison; Sermon 448 mentions that a Nigerian person's name was often connected with their tribe; Sermon 663 mentions that the right hand is the strong hand in Nigeria, the hand that gives and takes. Once, Nancy insulted a chef by taking food with her left hand. (See letter to parents, 5 Mar. 1967, for more details on this experience.); Sermon 705 says that Nigerians have a saying that two people can have 'hearts which beat together'. David related that theologically this is how Paul wanted to be with Jesus; Sermon 758 relates the functioning of a Nigerian meeting to select an elder; In sermon E38 David uses Biafra for the setting of an illustration on the importance of facts in the Christian faith; Sermons E47, E62 and 242 describe a funeral in a Nigerian village, evoking the finality of death; In sermon E76 David mentions that the Efik people name their pastor an 'Etubum'—the same name given to the man who beats the drum in a canoe to keep up the rhythm of those who paddle.

16. In Sermons 256, 420, 596 and 747 David mentions with astonishment that in Nigeria real change in society happened with a much smaller percentage of the population who called themselves 'Christian'; Sermon 258 mentions the efforts for evangelization in Nigeria; Sermon 274 mentions that Christian homes in Niegeria were much more orderly and clean than non-Christian homes; Sermon 303 mentions Mary Slessor and the beginnings of the work in Nigeria and the continual growth; Sermon 340 notes the story of a mature Nigerian elder who had an intuition about a dishonest candidate for

Interesting for their later life was a stop in Quebec City. In a newsletter from April 1968 they recounted their visit to the French congregations in Quebec:

> We particularly enjoyed our work in Quebec. French-speaking congregations seldom get an opportunity in Canada to hear missionaries because of the language barrier. Since Nancy is bilingual she was most warmly received. We greatly appreciate our warm welcome of the University of Sherbrooke as well as L'Eglise Reformer [sic] in Quebec City, Eglise St. Luc in Montreal and the L'Eglise des Cantons l'Est in Upper Melbourne.[17]

David had already begun to think about the following year's plans, particularly his desire to study church history and French somewhere in Europe. He was not sure where or when, so he was thankful for the advice of Dr. Jean Cruvellier, the pastor at St-Marc Church in Quebec City, who encouraged him to study in Paris.[18] Whether in Nigeria,

---

the ministry. The elder had a feeling that the young candidate was actually a member of a non-Christian secret society. In the end the elder's suspicions were well-founded and the student was rejected. David says that this gift of discerning the spirits could be of great use to the church (p. 5); Sermons 479 and E8 recounts David's meeting of Daniel Slessor, the adopted son of Mary Slessor. Daniel, a twin, was left for dead in the jungle (it was thought twins were bad luck). Mary found him, adopted him and now he is an elder in a church. David clearly saw the power of the Gospel in this story; In sermon 295 David relates how he learned to live with the Christians that God sent them and not simply the friends that they wanted to live with; In sermon 603 David explicitly contrasts the decline of the church in Europe and Canada with the growth of the church in Asia, Africa and Nigeria. Interestingly, he would often list continents *and* Nigeria for many years of his life. It is only near the end of his life when he became involved in missions in other African and southeast Asian countries that this focus on Africa was diminished. For example see sermons 552, 629, 632 and 636.

17. Newsletter to friends (3 Apr. 1968). [PCC Archives—File # 103-G-3.]

18. David Craig, letter to E.H. Johnson (4 Mar. 1968). [PCC Archives—File # 1990-5007-5-2.]

France or Switzerland, David prayed "that God will direct our affairs and make His way plain."[19]

NOW WHAT?

David and Nancy's long journey across Canada telling their stories took them all the way to Vancouver where they were finally confronted with the question, "now what"? Having completed his deputation work, David was still convinced he needed to study history and French, but was not yet sure this was the right time.[20] Likewise, Nancy had concerns of her own. In a letter to Remmelt Hummelen, program assistant for missionary education of the General Board of Missions, she wrote:

> Sometimes we get discouraged as we look to the future. More and more it seems impossible to return to Nigeria. How our hearts ache to return to those dear people! We are living in days of suspension which is a bit hard to take sometimes, but God will show us our plans in his good time.[21]

Amid this uncertainty, David and Nancy saw an interesting opportunity for short-term ministry while they were on the West coast.

In Vancouver David accepted a job offer to work as the youth pastor at Fairview Presbyterian Church. Because the political climate was still unsettled in Nigeria, the Board of World Missions granted David a short leave of absence and encouraged him to work in Vancouver on the condition that he be ready to return to Nigeria on six weeks notice.[22] E.H. Johnson had no problem loaning David and Nancy to Fairview for a short period of time, but he definitely wanted them back in Nigeria in

---

19. Newsletter to friends (3 Apr. 1968). [PCC Archives—File # 103-G-3.]

20. David Craig, letter to E.H. Johnson (21 Aug. 1968). [PCC Archives—File # 1990-5007-5-2.]

21. Nancy Craig, letter to C. Remmelt Hummelen (20 Dec. 1967). [PCC Archives—File# 103-G-3.]

22. See letter from E.H. Johnson to David (15 Oct. 1968). [PCC Archives—File # 1990-5007-5-2.]

the not too distant future. He wrote to David: "Certainly we want to be ready to help those people [the people of Nigeria] in this next difficult stage and you and Nancy are people equipped to make a particularly valuable contribution."[23]

Although it was short-lived, David and Nancy's time at Fairview was still significant. Fairview was a church with a long evangelical tradition which sought the kind of "vital Christianity" of which David had spoken in his seminary days.[24] In these years it was not common for the Presbyterian Church to appoint youth pastors, but the pastor of Fairview, the Reverend Dr. Ian Rennie, saw an excitement in David and Nancy which he wanted to share with the growing ranks of young adults and couples in his congregation. In a letter to E.H. Johnson, Rennie noted that David's "greatest contribution, of course, is just his presence in the life of the congregation which is a continual challenge to all of us to dedication and missionary service."[25]

For the next year Nancy and David dedicated themselves to the young people of the Fairview congregation, inviting them over almost every day for meals and conversation. David and Nancy's main responsibility was to facilitate the "Hi-teens" group and "College and Career" groups within the church. Also, they were involved in Friday night "Coffeehouse" meetings and in the Young Couples' Club.[26] If all this

---

23. E.H. Johnson to David Craig (15 Oct. 1968). [PCC Archives—File # 1990-5007-5-2.]

24. See Robert Burkinshaw, *Pilgrims in Lotus Land: Conservative Protstantism in British Columbia 1917-1981* (Kingston/Montreal: McGill-Queens University Press, 1995); Ian Rennie, "Conservatism in the Presbyterian Church in Canada in 1925 and beyond: an introductory exploration," *The Canadian Society of Presbyterian History Papers* (1982): 29-59.

25. Ian Rennie, letter to E.H. Johnson (3 Oct. 1968). [PCC Archives—File # 1990-5007-5-2.]

26. Many of their activites are described in their Christmas 1968 newsletter to family and friends.

activity was not enough, David also participated with Dr. Rennie in preaching, Bible studies and pastoral work.[27]

At the end of the year, however, the missions board of the denomination wanted David and Nancy to go back to Lagos to pastor a large congregation of the Presbyterian Church of Nigeria and a small expatriot church.[28] David took the position, but only on a short-term basis between July and December of 1969.[29]

At the end of their stay in Vancouver, David and Nancy noted the great progress that had been made during the past year. They were delighted that many of the students with whom they had been working had grown spiritually. Nancy recounted this story just a few days before they left:

> Dave's Thursday Bible Study group has really developed this winter and the kids are going to go on meeting together for study. They have become a closely knit group where each one feels free to discuss what is on his mind concerning his own discovery of Christ and to share problems. Just last night one of the fellows came to David smiling and said, 'I've finally really committed myself to Christ.' There couldn't be a better farewell gift.[30]

When David and Nancy left Vancouver on 19 June 1969 on a train across Canada, a large crowd of friends waved goodbye from the platform. One of these friends, Kit Somerville, would join them in September as a nurse with the Sudan Interior Mission in Port Harcourt.[31]

---

27. Examples of sermons preached at Fairview are: E29, E30 and E31.
28. Rodger Talbot, letter to David Craig (24 Jun. 1969). [PCC Archives—File # 1990-5007-5-2.]
29. See letter to friends (17 Jun. 1969).
30. Letter to friends (17 Jun. 1969).
31. Kit Somerville (now Schindell) also had many adventures on her trip to Africa. She wrote several beautiful letters to David and Nancy from the hospital at which she was working. In the letters she describes the terrible plight of the sick people in her war-torn area, but the tremendous joy she has

NIGERIA AGAIN

David arrived back in Nigeria to serve Lagos Presbyterian Church at the beginning of July 1969 (taking a trip through Holland on his way over). Nancy joined him at the end of August.[32] The church building, which was of modern design and low maintenance, was almost complete. Most of the circular building was made of non-painted cement with asbestos cement sheets used for roofing. One journalist wrote that once the project was entirely completed, this part of Lagos "will not only have one of the finest examples of modern ecclesiastical architecture in Africa but also a dynamic community centre designed to meet the spiritual and social needs of the people of that area."[33] David was one of the first pastors in this 'dynamic' building.

Life in this large suburban church was much different than life in Calabar. During his time in Lagos, David also aided those in the war-torn region of Biafra.[34] The work was draining, but stimulating. In October 1969, David wrote to the Mission Board about the progress and needs in the ministry:

---

in serving them. To get back to Lagos, Kit had to take a small cattle-boat. It was not a pleasant experience!

32. Nancy came later so that she could rest a bit and shake off a nasty cold before going to Africa. See letter to friends (17 Jun. 1969). See also letter of Nancy to the General Board of Missions (Jul. ?, 1969) ['?' intentional—it showed that she was relaxing and had lost track of the days.] [PCC Archives—File # 103-G-3.]

33. Paul Harrison, "A New Lagos Landmark: A look at an unusual experiment in church design," *Interlink: The Nigerian-American Quarterly Magazine* 5/2 (Apr.–Jn. 1969):2–3.

34. See letter to parents (27 Nov. 1969). When they returned David went to meet an elder of his old church Mr. Bassey. The last time Mr. Bassey had seen David, they were both prisoners. Mr. Bassey was sure that David had been killed and thrown into a river. When David came to the door, Mr. Bassey went grey thinking he was seeing a ghost, but when David assured him that he was really alive the whole Bassey family rejoiced with him and gave him a wonderful reception. They spent a joyful time discussing the plight of the Nigerian Church since David had left. Sermon E21.

We are extremely busy, involved and enjoying the work immensely. There has been considerable increase in the Ajegunle Congregation and also Victoria Island. The Yaba Congregation remains about the same size. Without any doubt it is most important that we have two men here as soon as it's possible. Otherwise it will be impossible either to grow or service the present needs here.[35]

Nancy too shared the joy and burden of working in Lagos by teaching at a local private grade-school.[36] The work was extremely hectic, but she enjoyed learning how to teach younger children.

Despite their intense involvement, David and Nancy did not feel led to continue working in Nigeria. Rather, they made plans to further David's education in church history and French in Europe. On their way to Europe on 1 January 1970 they stopped in the Canary Islands for a short, relaxing holiday.

---

35. David Craig, letter to Rodger Talbot (30 Oct. 1969). [PCC Archives—File # 1990-5007-5-2.]

36. Letter to parents (17 Oct. 1969).

CHAPTER SEVEN

A Student Again

IN THE SHADOW OF FAREL

Even before going back to Nigeria for the short contract from July to December 1969, David already clearly felt he needed to deepen his understanding of church history and the French language so he could better train to be a missionary in a French-speaking context.[1] To get this training, he and Nancy went to Neuchâtel, Switzerland, in January 1970 where David began doctoral studies on French Reformation history at the Neuchâtel Faculty of Protestant Theology.[2] Being in Neuchâtel allowed David to be constantly immersed in the French language and

---

1. Nancy had already paid David's school fees for January 1970 when she went through Neuchâtel in August 1969 on her way to Nigeria.
2. See letters of David to Board of World Missions. [PCC Archives—File # 103-F-3.] Importantly, David and Nancy were in a weak financial situation while studying in Switzerland. Earlier the Board of World Missions had made a cash advance to David after his departure from Calabar in 1967. Everything they owned was abandoned in Calabar because of the war. Rather than having to repay this debt, the Board agreed that the debt should be written off against war losses, thus freeing him of any responsibility for repayment. Earl F. Roberts, letter to David in Neuchatel (8 Sept. 1970). [PCC Archives—File # 103-G-3.]

also allowed him access to valuable research collections.[3]

David wanted to do his dissertation on the ecclesiology of French reformer Guillaume Farel. After finishing his course work, David had large reproductions made of a Farel text, but did not get past the initial stages of the research and writing of his dissertation.[4] Nevertheless, Farel interested David because he was French-speaking and perceived to be very dynamic in his missionary activity. Farel was a model of one who spoke up for the truth, held firm to the authority of Scripture and bowed before the sovereignty of God. Neuchâtel was where David did most of his studies, but during his time in Switzerland he would often visit Geneva and participate in conferences.[5]

While in Neuchâtel, David and Nancy often attended the Collégiale, the very church in which Guillaume Farel had served in the sixteenth century. During their stay, the pastor of the Collégiale, Rev. René Ariège, warmly welcomed them and appreciated David's evangelical fervour. With the support of Ariège, David became involved in training the young people of the church for profession of faith. Occasionally, however, David and Nancy would also visit an *Église libre*, a

---

3. David mentions that he sat under Prof. Philippe-H. Menoud who taught New Testament at Neuchâtel. Particularly David appreciated Prof. Menoud's teaching on the past, present and future aspects of the Kingdom of God. Sermon 283.

4. One presumes that the roughly 20-page manuscript (on size A4 paper) written on Farel found with his papers and sermons is the beginnings of his dissertation. David was very excited about the link between Farel and the other early French and German reformers. Much work has been done on Farel since the mid-1970s, but many of David's observations are still interesting and valid.

5. In September 1971 David went to Oxford in England for an international conference on patristics. Further, David returned to Switzerland in September of 1980 to attend a major colloquium on the life and thought of Farel. He is listed as a participant in the acts of the colloquium printed as: *Actes du colloque Guillaume Farel*, eds. Pierre Barthel, Rémy Scheurer and Richard Stauffer, Cahiers de la Revue de théologie et de philosophie, 9/I (Geneva/Lausanne/Neuchâtel, 1983), v.

A STUDENT AGAIN

more generally evangelical church not associated with the established Reformed churches.

Although he did not complete his doctoral thesis, the stories of the Reformation would become central to David's preaching and teaching. As previously noted, the stories of the Reformation were the only ones more important in his preaching than those from his life in Nigeria. It would be difficult to say how many times David mentioned various aspects of the Reformation, but references abound in his teaching. Most of the references are centered on the story of Martin Luther's conversion, the French Reformation (especially Jacques Lefèvre d'Etaples and Guillaume Farel) and the plight of the Huguenots. Yet in order to explain these he also had to study the Roman Catholic Church and the various Anabaptist groups of the 16th century.

WORK AND CHAPLAINCY

It was not easy financially for David and Nancy to live in Switzerland. With no full-time jobs, they had to do a great deal of part-time work to support their lives during these years. In order to be hired, Nancy needed to enroll as a student at the university because she was a foreigner.[6] With her student booklet signed by her professor at the beginning and end of each session, she was able to get employment. Nancy took secretarial jobs which included helping the registrar at the university, working for a lawyer, and, for the longest period of time, serving as secretary in the *service du contentieux* (Ministry of Transportation) in Neuchâtel. Nancy had learned how to type as a child but had never received formal secretarial training. The weekend before she began her first job, she borrowed a typewriter and typed all weekend to bring her speed up to the required number of words per minute for Monday morning!

David also needed to make some money. At first he took a job cleaning trains for the Swiss railway company. His co-workers were

---

6. Letter to friends (Mar. 1972).

astonished that a doctoral candidate would dirty his hands cleaning toilets. David did not mind so much—it gave him something to talk about. He also worked for several months in a watch shop helping to solder little metal pieces. More long-term, however, he became involved in campus ministries as assistant chaplain. He loved the position because it allowed him to get involved in students' lives.

As they did at Fairview in Vancouver, David and Nancy frequently invited students for conversation and dinner.[7] However, in Neuchâtel David ran into many skeptical students—this fairly frustrating in a city which had been one of the most important centres of Reformed theology in previous centuries.[8] Further frustration came from those who rejected their Reformed heritage and embraced the spirituality of a Hindu guru travelling the area seeking disciples. David remarked that the true nature of this guru's disciples was shown when they were stopped red-handed at the border of Switzerland with stolen jewellery. Disciples show their worth in their actions, argued David.[9]

As a chaplain, David also often had animated discussions with Marxist-leaning students or those who based their spiritual life principally on experience or emotion. In both cases he would try to prove to them the importance of the factuality of the Gospel message.[10] The faith of Christianity, said David to his fellow students, "is based on evidence *not* on emotional superstition."[11] Many students were attracted to David's call for vital Christianity. One student was so moved that he gave up extra scholarship money he had received to support the mission and relief work in Nigeria in which David and Nancy were previously involved.[12]

---

7. Sermon 230.

8. Sermon 691. Nancy and David's letter to friends of March 1972 and December 1973 give several examples of students with whom they worked.

9. Sermons 247, 292, 531.

10. Sermons 602 and 711.

11. Sermon E38.

12. Sermon 340.

A STUDENT AGAIN

TRAVELS AND EDIFICATION

David and Nancy profited fully from the beautiful scenery surrounding them in Switzerland. They would often spend time in the mountains enjoying exhilarating hikes.[13] David's *joie de vivre* was evident to the new friends he and Nancy had made there. They were surprised that he wanted to know so much about the small country of Switzerland even though he came from such a large country like Canada. Further, they were impressed with his genuine curiosity about everything Swiss—especially fine wines, cheese and chocolate. He and Nancy would guard this special link with Switzerland and their Swiss friends for the rest of their lives.

Being in Switzerland provided them with opportunities to visit other parts of Europe. In the spring of 1973, David and Nancy, with several friends, set out to visit Romania to participate in an Orthodox Easter ceremony. This was a complicated endeavour, however, because Romania was a Communist-controlled country and these were the years of the Cold War. Yet David and Nancy participated in the clandestine work of transporting Bibles into the country. They had a few dozen Bibles which they were to give to a contact in Bucharest. At the border they were nervous, but everything went smoothly. Their Bibles were received gratefully by their contact, and they witnessed the historic rituals of the Eastern Orthodox Church. During the short visit, David and his friends had the opportunity to meet the head of the Orthodox Church in Romania—a man who did not share their evangelical fervour and reminded them that they need not bring any more Bibles in his country.[14]

David also visited l'Abri during his time in Switzerland. In 1955 the Schaeffer family established l'Abri as a Christian community which, although neither a retreat centre, nor a commune, nor a seminary,

---

13. Sermon 543.
14. Letter to friends (Dec. 1973).

incorporated elements from all of these.¹⁵ Francis Schaeffer, the founder of l'Abri, was a Presbyterian minister from Pennsylvania who had done several years of seminary education under Cornelius Van Til and J. Gresham Machen, two important conservative Presbyterian thinkers in America. Schaeffer, a prolific author whose brand of apologetics complemented that of John Warwick Montgomery, was clearly opposed to theological modernism and promoted an orthodox Protestant faith armed by a moderate presuppositional approach to Christian apologetics—both of which David appreciated.¹⁶ Throughout the rest of his career David would often cite Schaeffer with great appreciation.

David and Nancy visited l'Abri regularly, sometimes as frequently as two Sundays a month, during their time in Switzerland. They often sat at the same table as Dr. Schaeffer, listening to and participating in the discussions. At one point, Nancy asked Dr. Schaeffer why his books were not being translated into French. He was in French Switzerland, yet the French had limited exposure to his theological writings. So, Nancy took it upon herself, with Schaeffer's permission, to translate one of Dr. Schaeffer's books titled *He is There and He is Not Silent*.¹⁷

By mid-1975 David knew that he could find work in Switzerland, but he and Nancy felt the tug to work in Quebec more strongly. Hence, the couple, along with their first child, moved back to Canada in December 1975. Their voyage home was the most memorable voyage of their lives—not for happy reasons. They wanted to celebrate their return trip, so they decided to enjoy a nice, relaxed 'cruise' across the ocean aboard the TS/S Stephan Batory. The ship, a spry 23 years old in 1975, had been purchased by Polish Ocean Lines from Holland America

---

15. See: Edith Schaeffer, *L'Abri* (Wheaton, Il.: Tyndale House, 1969).

16. Later in life David cut out and copied an article by Shaeffer on American Presbyterianism. David greatly enjoyed the article and made many copies to give to friends. Francis Shaeffer, "Shaeffer Reflects on 50 Years of Denominational Ins & Outs." *Christianity Today* 25/7 (10 Apr. 1981): 28-30.

17. See letter to friends (Dec. 1973). The work was published as: Francis Schaeffer, *Dieu - ni silencieux ni lointain* (Editions Telos, 1979), 111pp.

A STUDENT AGAIN

Lines in 1968 and refitted and renamed (it was formerly called the Maasdam IV). It was one of the last regularly-scheduled trans-Atlantic passenger lines in existence. Although the ship was relatively comfortable, the weather on the North Atlantic was very unsettled. The trip, which lasted ten days, was plagued by sickness and misery! What had promised to be a relaxing and restful ten days turned out to be totally wretched. Needless to say, when the Craigs saw the Chateau Frontenac of Quebec City, built on a giant, immovable rock, they were overjoyed. David would often compare the longing that he had to be on that immovable rock after the turbulence at sea with the longing a Christian ought to have for the stability of life in God.[18]

---

18. Sermons 105, 465 and 513.

CHAPTER EIGHT

Evangelism and the Église Catholique Réformée

MISSION AND THE ÉGLISE ST-MARC

Back in Canada David was asked to take over as pastor in the French-speaking St-Marc Presbyterian Church in Quebec City in January 1976. Although a small minority by the mid-1970s, French-speaking Protestants were not entirely new to Quebec.[1] Several of the first governors of New France were Huguenots and until the arrival of the Jesuits in 1625, Reformed believers were influential in the colony's daily life.[2] It was the Jesuits who began systematic and persistent exclusion of the Reformed believers.[3] At the time the English gained control of the lower St. Lawrence and New France in 1759, there was no public witness of Protestantism in Francophone culture. The few remaining Reformed believers then began attending worship with

---

1. See Marc-André Bédard, *Les Protestants en Nouvelle-France* (Quebec: La Société Historique de Québec, 1978); Jean-Louis Lalonde, *Des loups dans la bergerie: Les Protestants de Langue Française au Québec. 1534–2000* (Montreal: Fides, 2002).

2. Marcel Trudel, *Histoire de la Nouvelle France*. Vol. 1 (Montreal: Fides, 1963), ch. IV; Lalonde, *Des Loups*, 28.

3. Carole Blackburn, *Harvest of Souls: The Jesuit Missions and Colonialism in North America 1632–1650* (Montreal and Kingston: McGill-Queen's University Press, 2000), 27; Bédard, *Les Protestants*, 15.

English Protestants who permitted religious freedom.[4]

In 1835 Swiss missionaries arrived with the hope that they could also proclaim the gospel to French-speaking Roman Catholic Canadians.[5] This missionary work came to fruition with an established parish in 1837. Sometime later the Swiss missionary society terminated its work and The Presbyterian Church in Canada took up the challenge. By 1880, 25 parishes along with many schools had been established.[6]

The Presbyterian Church in Canada, however, began to lose interest in sustaining mission work in Quebec and turned its attention to the rapidly developing West. By 1922 there were but nine French Presbyterian churches remaining in Quebec. After the Canadian church union of 1925, even fewer resources were available for French work in Quebec within the Presbyterian churches that remained out of the union.[7] By 1975 only three Francophone parishes were active in The Presbyterian Church in Canada—Église St-Luc in Montreal, Église St-Paul in Melbourne and Église St-Marc in Ste-Foy (then a suburb of Quebec City). Mission work was started in the region of Quebec City in the 1950s under Armand Jossinet and new momentum was gained with the coming of the Rev. Prof. Jean Cruvellier to Quebec in 1963.[8] The mission was officially established as a church in early 1967. After

---

4. Dominique Vogt-Raguy, "Les Communautés Protestants Francophones au Québec. 1834-1925," Ph.D diss. (l'Université Michel de Montaigne-Bordeaux III, 1996), 36ff.; René Hardy, *Contrôle social et mutation de la culture religieuse au Québec 1830–1939* (Montreal: Boréal, 1999), 20ff.

5. René Paquin, "Les protestants canadiens-français et le 'réveil' catholique dans le Québec du XIXe siècle: brève hsitoire d'une concurrence," in: *l'Identité des protestants francophones au Québec: 1834–1997*, ed. Remon, Denis (Montreal: Acfas, 1998), 81; Vogt-Raguy, "Les Communautés," 40ff.; Hardy, *Contrôle social*, 30ff.

6. See also Jean-Louis Lalonde, *Belle-Rivière, 1840-2006* (Montreal: Société d'histoire du protestantisme franco-québécois, 2007).

7. Vogt-Raguy, "Les Communautés," 924.

8. See Ross Davidson, "Mission au Québec Hier: Entrevue avec le Pasteur Armand Jossinet," *La Vie Chrétienne* (May 1988): 6, 10.

Rev. Sadi Mezaour's short and difficult tenure with the parish in the early 1970s, Rev. Ross Davidson brought some stability to it.[9] Davidson, however, took a call to the Presbyterian work in Richmond in 1975 prompting the church in Quebec to call David.

David accepted the call to the church and presided his first service as pastor on 11 January 1976. He was installed officially as pastor on 12 February.[10] St-Marc Church was at first comprised of a number of French-speaking European immigrants, but soon attracted a diverse array of university students with the help of two Navigator outreach workers.[11] Not without some resistance, David encouraged the church to become more Quebecois. He sought Quebecois leadership and music, and this attracted a large number of university students from nearby Laval University.[12] Many of the new adherents were children of *révolution tranquille* parents—many were on the left of the political spectrum and had sympathy towards separatism. Yet under David's leadership they were gathered together in a common cause.

Interestingly, although many of this young generation rejected what they perceived as the previous generation's monolithic conservative Catholicism, they did not reject 'religion' or 'spirituality' as such. In fact, in many university settings there was great interest in becoming involved with religions and spirituality of all kinds. Further, universi-

---

9. For a very brief history of Presbyterian work in Quebec City after 1925 see: Jean Porret, "Les francophones dans l'Église presbytérienne au Canada, *La Vie Chrétienne*" (Sept. 1984): 9.

10. David and Nancy were welcomed to Quebec in *La Vie Chrétienne* (Nov/Dec/Jan 1975–76): 7; and again (this time with photo) in (Feb. 1976): 1.

11. This increase in student-oriented activities was seen in the news given in *La Vie Chrétienne* during these years. See the news concerning St-Marc in *La Vie Chrétienne* 27/1 (Jan. 1978): 11.

12. David rejoiced in both the church's student presence and multi-ethnic make-up. In sermon 731 he said that the church had some French-speakers, Germans, Swiss, a Romanian, a few Americans and 'I find that it is great that God has even chosen a Dutchman—Martin Geleynse, as the co-ordinator of our theological seminary."

ties actively renewed their academic interest in studying religion and the Bible.[13] Students seemed to have a great thirst to know what they thought had been hidden from their parents' generation.

David was well-prepared to work with university students. Many people noted his 'winsome' or 'happy-go-lucky' attitude. Although he was very flexible with many people (and the clock), he often made one forget that he was unprepared or late by his laughter and enthusiasm. It was often very helpful for him to have a wife who was a fair bit more punctual and organized than he was. Nancy complemented him throughout his life and ministry. She made up for some of his 'overly flexible' habits.

Both David and Nancy believed being with people was one of the most important keys in their missionary method. They saw that a strong relationship with God was greatly facilitated by strong relationships with other Christians. For this reason they became 'spiritual parents' for many young folk seeking more understanding of Scripture and how to live the Christian life. David knew that the scriptural message of new birth was not a simple, irrational decision, but something which took certain people a great deal of time to digest and process. Hence, he was willing to accompany them throughout this new life.

Many young couples responded favourably to this message in the years around 1980, and the church grew considerably. Nancy speaks of the changes in the church to friends in a newsletter:

> The work at Eglise St-Marc naturally consumes most of our energy and fills most of our conversation. The little congregation of five years ago has grown into a little bigger congregation of about sixty adults. Our Sunday School now has enough children to divide them into five different classes with two team teachers each. And our nursery is bursting at its seams with fifteen babies between 0 and 3 years![14]

---

13. Moir, *A History of Biblical Studies in Canada*, 83.
14. Letter to friends (May 1980).

PROMOTING THE REFORMATION

In dealing with all the new members in the church, David soon saw the need for the kind of knowledge he had gained in Switzerland. His young congregation needed to know that they were rooted in a firm historical basis. Not only was David's preaching based on Scripture, the ultimate authority, but it was also faithful to the long French Reformed legacy. David was greatly concerned with connecting his young French-speaking congregation members to the larger history of French-speaking Protestantism. It was always his argument that a Reformed church was vitally French and not simply an English import.[16]

David travelled a great deal in these years teaching individuals and groups what it meant to be 'Reformed'. In fact, although his church was officially Presbyterian, it was commonly known in French as the *Église réformée St-Marc*.[17] After the 16th century Reformation, the churches in Scotland were called Presbyterian, but in Holland, France and Switzerland (among others) they were called Reformed. But though there was a difference in name, these churches were all in agreement on a general understanding of the message of Scripture. In the 16th and 17th centuries, for example, these churches often sent delegates to each

---

15. For the positive and negative results of growth see David and Nacy's letter to friends (Jun. 1982). "The growth of a congregation goes hand-in-hand with a lack of space, misunderstandings, disappointments and personality conflicts; it also brings meetings, visits, conversations, telephone calls and less time for reflection and relaxation for us as a couple or as a family" [translation mine].

16. From this vision one understands David's active participation in the Huguenot Society of Canada. See *Huguenot Trails* 23/3 (Fall 1994): 4.

17. In an undated photo (pre-1988) one can make out the sign in front of the Church as reading "St-Marc Église présbyterienne réformée."

other's church meetings and remained in close contact. Some, even before David's time, thought that it might be more helpful to refer to the church as 'reformed' in Quebec because in Francophone Europe the churches went under this name. David certainly thought that the name of the churches might change from one country to another, but they all held to a Reformed theology.

David was particularly concerned about imparting to his young church members the idea that the 'Reformed' Church was not an aberration, but a faithful continuation of God's Church. It was a faithful form of a real *catholic* church in opposition to the *Roman* Catholic Church predominant in Quebec. David did not want his church to be simply called the *Église Réformée*, but the "Église *Catholique* Réformée" to emphasise this continuity with the *good* tradition of Catholicism before the Reformation.[18] In a certain sense, one could argue that David thought the Roman Catholic Church appropriated and perverted the word 'Catholic' to refer only to itself. Many of David's colleagues appreciated this concern, but found the word 'Catholic' too loaded to use in official signs and documents.[19] In any case, David's concern was to highlight that a Reformed church was not simply a foreign imposition, but in the good tradition of Quebec.[20] He always wanted the French speakers to make the Reformed church their own.

---

18. See the notes from his course "Ordre et Discipline Ecclésiastique" which he taught at the Institut Farel: "The reformers were very conscious of their debt to the past. So, they tried to 'reform' (not separate from), but reform the church according to the authority of the Word which clearly implied a form of church government and the authority of that government" [translation mine].

19. See letters of l'Église chrétienne réformée de Beauce (15 Oct. 1987) and l'Église St-Marc (31 Oct. 1987). The name of the future denomination was much debated in the C.E.R.Q. meetings until the name "l'Église Réformée du Québec" was chosen at the meeting in March 1988 (C.E.R.Q. PV.880304): 6.

20. David actively promoted the work of Marc-André Bédard who wrote an important master's thesis on the presence of Huguenots in New France. Marc-André Bédard, *Les Protestants en Nouvelle-France* (Quebec: La Société

EVANGELISM AND THE ÉGLISE CATHOLIQUE RÉFORMÉE

In these early years, David started teaching general theological education courses in the basement of his house. Having a long-term impact on the Quebecois necessitated the availability of careful and thoughtful theological reflection. Soon this theological work evolved into the Institut Farel when other Reformed pastors and missionaries combined their different works.

To promote this unity and the work in Quebec, David often travelled many kilometres to preach or teach or give presentations about the French work. Nancy wrote of these frequent road trips in May 1980:

> David (and I occasionally with him) has been off around the country quite a bit these last years. Many of our Presbyterian congregations are interested in Quebec and in the French ministry here. They have invited David to numerous mission week-ends to tell about St-Marc, what is being done in the province and what is the future for the Presbyterian work here. The church at large needs to have a new understanding of what it means and will mean in the future to be a minister or a congregation in Quebec. Living, ministering and evangelism here are very different from that done in the rest of Canada. One must be taught to really see this as a mission field. He is an excellent ambassador for Quebec.[21]

What is interesting about Nancy's commentary is not only that David was often away from his home church, but also how Nancy (and, presumably David) viewed the nature and future of French Reformed work. First, one notes that they clearly saw the work in Quebec as 'different' from that in the rest of Canada. Second, despite the large needs, they were quite optimistic about the future of the Reformed work—in their minds the work was only beginning.

Much of the vitality of St-Marc Church turned around the 'Koinonia' groups which gathered weekly to discuss Scripture and build relationships. These groups were an important aspect in David's missionary

---

Historique de Québec, 1978).
21. Letter to friends (May 1980).

method. He not only wanted those frequenting his church to listen to him preach on Sunday morning, but he also wanted them to participate in each other's lives. 'Kononia', a Greek word meaning 'community' (especially that of Christians in the Spirit) was fitting to describe the kind of vibrant, relationship-building communities that David felt were helpful for growth in spiritual life. Many others beside David led these groups in these years, but David was very active in promoting the groups and led at least one every session. With the courses at Farel, prayer meetings, new members meetings, on top of these Koinonia meetings, David's schedule was quite full.

Much of the activity at St-Marc Church centred on the diffusion and explanation of Scripture. David knew that the kind of vital faith he wished to promote needed to be based on Scripture. To highlight the importance of the Bible in the life of the Christian, David helped to organize the distribution of 10,000 Bibles on the campus of Laval University. Financing for the project was secured at the last minute, but all the Bibles were taken in a relatively short period of time.[22] More generally, David's focus on the availability of Scripture was highlighted in his continuing participation in the *Société Biblique Canadienne*.[23]

David saw that many other evangelicals were not concerned about the type of biblical and doctrinal education he wanted to promote. Rather, they employed a simplistic biblical hermeneutic and relied very heavily on their spiritual experience as their guide in life. The late 1970s and early 1980s were a time of explosive growth for experientially-based evangelical churches.[24] Many young Quebecois men and women were not content with the form of Catholicism that had dominated Quebec for the past century, and now looked elsewhere for more satisfying

---

22. See sermons 318, E35 and news of the St-Marc Church in *La Vie Chrétienne* 27/1 (Jan. 1978): 11.

23. In news of St-Marc Church, *La Vie Chrétienne* (Mar. 1982): 2.

24. See Richard Lougheed, Wesley Peach and Glenn Smith, eds. *Histoire du Protestantisme au Québec depuis 1960: Une Analyse Anthropologique, Culturelle et Historique* (Quebec: La Clarière, 1999), esp. ch. 2.

spiritual options. Although some would go much further into spiritism and the occult, a significant number were drawn to the intense spiritual emotionalism present in certain evangelical churches. These churches were much more experience-based than other traditional Protestant churches, yet they still shared a Christian vocabulary and sought to have a biblical foundation.

Because these more emotion-driven churches were so strong among young, French-speaking former Catholics (i.e. among the same people with whom David was working), David felt compelled to consider the strengths and weaknesses of this movement more closely. For example, he wrote and spoke a great deal about the excesses in the Charismatic movement. It was not simply that he wanted to be a stick-in-the-mud conservative Protestant, but that he was convinced by his reading of Scripture that a movement such as this was unhealthy for the church in the long run. Particularly, these sorts of movements inevitably bred doctrinal confusion and disunity in the church.[25]

COORDINATING THE MINISTRY

The threat of disunity was very real for David. For this reason, from the time he arrived in Quebec he took great interest in coordinating French-Reformed mission work. Rather than simply watch as everyone 'did their own thing', he wanted to work together with other like-minded missionaries as much as possible.

For example, David encouraged other church plants. In 1979 several Quebecois families in St-Georges-de-Beauce met with David to inquire about forming a Reformed church (i.e. Presbyterian church). These young families were recent university graduates who were involved in the Navigators campus ministry as students. Upon their return to the Beauce they felt the need to organise their work. Under the oversight of David and Eglise St-Marc, they formed a church and called Guy Dubé,

---

25. See sermon E42.

and, subsequently, Jean Zoellner, to be their pastor.[26] Further, David heartily encouraged Doug and Sylvie Sparks, a young married couple at St-Marc Church, to start a new church in the Baie-Comeau area in September 1983.[27] The project did not work as well as Doug and Sylvie might have liked, but David strongly encouraged their initiative and desire to plant new churches.

David's focus on the methods and objectives of the French mission work in the Presbyterian Church was clearly evident early on in his work at St-Marc Church. In February 1978, David wrote an article for *The Presbyterian Record* which outlined what he considered to be the foundations and the objectives of mission work in Quebec.[28] First, he clearly linked the Reformed work among the Quebecois with the Huguenots and the long history of the French Reformed movement. Second, he linked the present post-"Quiet Revolution" situation in Quebec with that of the Reformation. These links led him to an obvious conclusion:

> Now, why mention all this? Well, historically it is in these moments of tremendous upheaval, where the old structures are breaking up and the old roots cut, that God seems to work most dramatically. Men sense their rootlessness and search for reality and in some remarkable way seem more open to the Son of God. I believe we are living in a period of unparalleled opportunity for the gospel . . . right here in our own country![29]

---

26. See the testimony of one of the founding members of the St-Georges Church, Luc Thibaudeau in "Cote des Neiges Report," *Channels* 1/2 (Winter 1984): 4-5. See also "Une Entrevue avec une famille de St-Georges de Beauce," *La Vie Chrétienne* 30 (Jul./Aug. 1981): 15

27. See "Cote des Neiges Report," *Channels* 1/2 (Winter 1984): 3–4; *Minutes of Synod of Quebec and Eastern Ontario* (19 Oct. 1984), 17.

28. David Craig, "[De] Québec avec Amour!" *Presbyterian Record* (Feb. 1978): 10-11. In French: "De Québec avec Amour," *La Vie Chrétienne* 27 (Jun./Jul./Aug. 1978): 3, 10, 12.

29. Craig, "[De] Québec avec Amour!" 11.

In these few comments we see David making the case for increased work in Quebec. Not only is it the continuation of earlier French Reformed ministry, but now is the time to do it, argued David.

These same themes of hope and opportunity had already come to the fore in David's report for the mission committee of the Synod of Quebec and Eastern Ontario in October 1977.[30] An important question posed to this synod was the feasibility of a French-speaking Presbytery within The Presbyterian Church in Canada. After studying the question for a year, however, it was decided that a standing committee on French ministries would be better.[31]

Besides the French ministries committee, David got together on 5 September 1978 with a number of other pastors and leaders interested in promoting French-speaking Reformed activity in the town of Montmorency, to draw up and sign a common agreement. The group was known as the Alliance Réformée Évangélique (A.R.E.) and their agreement, the "Manifeste de Montmorency."[32] In thirteen articles the agreement underlined the foundation of Scripture, the centrality of Jesus Christ and the importance of conversion and action in the Christian life. However, the agreement did not speak clearly about matters of church structure or details of denominational affiliation.[33] The group could agree to general principles of Reformed theology, but represented a number of different denominations.

The *Manifeste* was a public profession of their founding principles, but they also had points of action. It its beginning the Alliance had roughly five main objectives:

---

30. *Minutes of Synod of Quebec and Eastern Ontario* (21 Oct. 1977): 24–25.

31. *Minutes of Synod of Synod of Quebec and Eastern Ontario* (20 Oct. 1978): 18–20.

32. Text available as: "Manifeste de Montmorency; déclaration de foi," *Parole* 1/1 (1979): 9–11.

33. See especially article thirteen on 'discrimination', "Manifeste de Montmorency," *Parole* 1/1 (1979): 11.

1. To promote unity among Christians with Reformed theological convictions (it was not yet clear exactly what this unity might look like)
2. To promote the spread of the biblical message among Francophones by whatever practical method was helpful (i.e. organizing financial aid, promoting radio ministry, etc.)
3. To begin a journal of biblical and theological reflection (*Parole* magazine)
4. To publish or reedit Reformed works in the French language (les éditions *Parole*)
5. To aid in the formation of a full-orbed Reformed theological seminary

These objectives were all fulfilled in the coming years with varied amounts of success. As ideas were more clearly formed, new participants enthusiastically joined, but several of the original members no longer felt comfortable continuing—especially when the Alliance more clearly defined the church structure and confession related to the first main objective.

For his part, David was intimately involved in the fifth objective of the Alliance. On several occasions he published substantial articles in the journal *Parole* (edited by Daniel Racine),[34] but his main work was in preaching and teaching biblical, Reformed theology. His independent theological school was soon transformed into the Institut Farel in cooperation with the Alliance.[35] This modest theological faculty was greatly aided by the coming of Rev. Martin Geleynse as coordinator and

---

34. David would serve as chief editor of *Parole* magazine in 1985 and 1986.

35. Contrary to what one might think, it was actually John Miller, the teacher of biblical languages at Farel and not David (who had done doctoral work on Farel), who suggested that the institution be called "Farel" after the 16th-century French Reformer. The dynamism in these early years at Farel is represented in: Harold Kallemeyn, "Reformed Theological Training in Quebec City?" *The Banner* (1 Jun. 1981): 11.

dean.[36] An important initiative which never came to fruition was to link up Farel with the theological program at Laval University.[37] In these years David continued to teach ecclesiology, biblical theology, systematic theology and, of course, church history. Although Rev. Geleynse had to depart from the Institut Farel for health reasons in 1986, it continued on under the able leadership of Rev. Jean-Guy deBlois.[38]

Throughout the early 1980s David fought to have the Institut Farel recognized and supported by all levels of The Presbyterian Church in Canada. He would often do presentations for Farel and the French work in individual congregations across Canada. Further, the Renewal Fellowship within The Presbyterian Church in Canada raised quite a bit of money for David and the Institut Farel. Almost annually, David brought projects before the Presbytery of Quebec, the Synod of Quebec and Eastern Ontario and even the General Assembly. He was fairly successful at attracting funding from Presbyterian sources for Farel,[39] but

---

36. Martin Geleynse's 1984 article in *Channels* captures much of the enthusiasm and vision of the participants in the *Institut Farel* at this time. "Q. How Do You Spell 'Miracle'? A. F-A-R-E-L," *Channels* 1/2 (Winter 1984): 5-6.

37. See "Compte rendu de la 1ère réunion du comité de programme et de supervision Université du Québec-Institut Farel," (22 Mar. 1985).

38. *Minutes of General Assembly ARE-Farel* (1 Mar. 1986).

39. A significant source of annual funding was through the *Robert Fund* administered by the synod of Quebec and Eastern Ontario. For example, see *Minutes of Synod of Quebec and Eastern Ontario* (15-16 Oct. 1982): Appendix E; (19 Oct. 1984): 37. Further, approval was given by General Assembly to give a major annual grant to Farel starting in 1983 based on a recommendation from Mr. A. McLean. See *The Acts and Proceedings of the One Hundred and Ninth General Assembly of The Presbyterian Church in Canada* (1983): 36. This grant was contested on several grounds at the 1984 General Assembly. *Acts and Proceedings of General Assembly* (1984): 25, 202. An amendment by A.D. MacLeod to the contestation of the grant, stated that "the 110th Assembly received this information [i.e. that the grant was not going to be paid out] with regret."

he could not gain the full approval of the denomination for its theological curriculum.[40]

The creation of this 'new' church alliance was troublesome to some who saw the limited evangelical landscape already full of imported Protestant denominations.[41] For this reason David needed to defend his involvement in its establishment. For example, through his uncle, Dr. Arthur Hill, David heard of some trenchant critique of this new work—critique to which he needed to respond:

> Several things in [the critic's] letter need a word of explanation. I fail to see where [the Reformed evangelical Alliance] is 'scripturally wrong, psychologically bad and practically adding to the confusion of Christendom.' I've been finding exactly the opposite on all three counts. I genuinely feel that a sound Reformed position answers in the greatest way possible the challenge of the Roman Church. Québec's roots are Reformed. We're not adding or creating anything! We're building on historical and biblical roots. The interest confirms this![42]

In this response we see several of the key themes David would continually repeat; among the evangelicals, the Reformed hold the most appropriate response to the spiritual situation of Quebec, the Reformed presence is not something 'new', and the "proof is in the pudding". Having a clear conscience, David went forward in his work for the Alliance.

PADRE CRAIG

The work in Quebec City was not easy financially for David and his young family (another beautiful child had been added to their family while there), so David also took a position as a chaplain in the

---

40. *Acts and Proceedings of General Assembly* (1982): 89, 217-218, 389; (1983): 36–37; (1985): 300.
41. Sermon E42.
42. Letter to Arthur Hill, Ste-Foy (22 Feb. 1979).

Canadian military. In university he was already enrolled in the C.O.T.C. (Canadian Officer Training Corps) and served as assistant padre. When he came to Quebec in 1976, he began work as a chaplain at a military base north of Quebec City for a time, but also at Gagetown, New Brunswick, Trenton, Ontario, Comox, British Colombia and even Lahr, Germany. He was not just a desk jockey, but actively participated in training exercises. Besides the financial stability this sideline job provided for his family, it also presented a wonderful opportunity to minister. He loved the camaraderie he enjoyed with the other soldiers and answered a great need in helping the families of those sent out to serve overseas.

David also recognized the need for a strong evangelical presence in the armed forces. He thought that much of the chaplaincy work had degenerated to that of a social worker; so he focused more of his efforts on evangelism. His messages to the soldiers were most often a call for biblical renewal and an expression of faith. By studying David's style in his sermons for these occasions, one gets the impression that those in his audience knew something of Christianity, but were not deeply rooted in it. Hence, his call was to develop a nominal Christianity into a vital and deep faith.[43] Notice how he confronts his listeners at CFB Kingston in 1999:

> But now that Jesus was contradicting their personal points of view, their opinions, their visions and their perception of things, he was intolerable!
>
> How many good Canadian people who attend church (even if it is only at Christmas and Easter), people who call themselves 'Christians', are at the same point 'turned off', even shocked by what Jesus says and by what he demands? It is not that they do not understand Jesus—it is that they understand him only too well, and refuse his message!

---

43. Sermons 176, 738, 751, E2, E3, E4, E88, E89, E90, E91, E93.

Is it not somewhat true in varying degrees with all of us? When our ideas are challenged, when what Jesus says conflicts with what we think or with our opinions, we react! We 'rationalise' what Jesus has said. Perhaps it is a certain habit or past time that we love, what videos we watch, how we treat our friends and families, what we want to buy or not buy, what our approach to our work is, etc. All of these can come into conflict with what Jesus asks of us.[44]

David's goal of this confrontation with nominal Christianity was always to highlight the importance of Christ's teaching and his grace. He confronted the soldiers with Scripture's testimony because he wanted to be faithful to what he felt was God's call.[45]

Further, David aimed particularly to promote the work of French Protestant chaplains. Until that time French Canadians were almost exclusively served by Roman Catholic chaplains. David felt that Protestants should also have a chance to give biblical encouragement and counsel to the French-speaking soldiers. He received some resistance from others in the Armed Forces who did not share this concern, but he did help at least three or four Protestant ministers to become directly engaged in this French chaplaincy.[46]

His work in the army, however, was not simply an outgrowth of his work in the parish. Actually, the army often provided him with enthusiasm for his work back home. He loved working with soldiers and often used his experiences with them to enrich his teaching in his regular church duties.[47] His passion for work in the military remained throughout his life. He served the army as chaplain on several bases in Ontario

---

44. Sermon E2 "Jesus' Basic Test."

45. In sermon 196 David relates that the experiences of the faithful chaplain the military is somewhat like the experiences of the Huguenots who stood up to the king and government of France in the 17th century. When there is resistance to God's message it should make us more dependent on God.

46. Several years after David's death, Nancy generously donated David's 'mess kit' (ie. his official chaplain's uniform) to a new Protestant chaplain working north of Quebec City.

47. See Sermons 113, 196, 399, 650 and 744.

and Quebec until his death. In the end he achieved the rank of major and was chosen as an *aide-de-camp* (official personal assistant) of the lieutenant governor of Quebec, the Honourable Lise Thibault.[48]

ST-MARC TO ST-MATTHIEU

The work at St-Marc Church grew steadily, and the little building housing the church was often full to overflowing. Because of its proximity to Laval University there were many visiting students and families. Jean Porret, editor of *La Vie Chrétienne*, wrote his impressions of the young church in 1980:

> There is truly a rich and active life that I would like to describe. I was surprised by the youth and number of young people who have joined the church in the last year. Clearly, in reading over the activities of the Church at the end of this journal you will realize that there are many and they are well attended, so much so that sometimes the church is almost too small to hold everyone. From the men's prayer group to the Bible studies for different categories of Christians, there is a place for everyone ... The pastor and leadership team put heavy emphasis on evangelisation and teaching. Hence, the different groups in the parish offer to everyone the opportunity to know about and grow in the faith.[49]

At the time the work and interest seemed limitless—all that slowed it down was the lack of qualified French pastors and financing for their work. David saw a great harvest, but few workers.[50] Consequently, he pushed even more for support.[51]

---

48. Ms. Thibault came to David's funeral in Oct. 2001 and said some kind words about David's life and faith. See her contribution in "A la mémoire de David Trevor Craig, 1937–2001," *En Lui*, Numéro spécial (mars 2002): 11..

49. J. Porret, "Une Église jeune qui grandit: St-Marc à Québec," *La Vie Chrétienne* 29 (Oct. 1980): 4–5 [translation mine].

50. Sermon 284 [translation mine].

51. See reports on French mission in *Minutes of Synod of Quebec and Eastern Ontario* (17 Oct. 1980): 23–25; (16 Oct. 1981): 39; (15–16 Oct. 1982):

As mentioned, David worked with many other smaller groups during his time in Quebec City. One of the groups was a small gathering in Trois-Rivières, a significant industrial centre on the north shore of the St. Lawrence River between Quebec City and Montreal. He believed that missionary activity should focus on this main corridor between Montreal and Quebec. A group from Trois-Rivières wanted him to become involved in their work. He said that he would come and be their pastor if they could get ten faithful people together. They did, so in June 1984 he left Quebec City with Nancy and his two children to be the group's full-time pastor.[52]

David and Nancy had many questions when they arrived in Trois-Rivières. This time they did not have a manse beside a church in which to live—everything had to be built from scratch. David felt that if he was to teach his students at Farel the necessity of church planting, then he should lead by example. St-Marc was stable enough to go on its own, but the small group in Trois-Rivières really needed leadership. David decided that this was a good time to move on. The work in Quebec needed to progress, and was progressing! Nancy, sharing David's vision, wrote to friends about this progression:

> When we arrived back in Quebec City eight years ago, there were only three Reformed parishes in the province, now there are eight—three in Montreal, one in Melbourne, in St-Georges-de-Beauce, in Ste-Foy, in Ste-Croix and in Trois-Rivières AND a Reformed Faculty of Theology (Institut Farel) AND our first Quebecois minister and four candidates for the ministry AND an Alliance that joins us all together. We are excited as we watch God work![53]

David and Nancy saw the work in Quebec advancing and work in Trois-Rivières at the cutting edge.

Appendix C.
    52. See *La Vie Chrétienne* (Oct./Nov. 1984): 16.
    53. Letter to friends (Autumn 1984).

EVANGELISM AND THE ÉGLISE CATHOLIQUE RÉFORMÉE

Eight years after the work had begun in Trois-Rivières, David commented on its beginnings in a sermon dealing with God's blessing on his work. He remembered that the work began with Bible studies in the office of one of the participants. At first a number of people were interested in the studies, but once he began dealing with the more prickly subjects of sin and the fall, the participation dropped by half. Rather than become discouraged, David, the happy optimist, quipped that he guessed "those of the half that left were not sinners."[54] David continued on and slowly more people joined the congregation.

David also saw God's providence in the search for a house with a living room spacious enough to accommodate a small worshipping group. David and Nancy had their eye on a house for sale in Trois-Rivières, but it was too costly. After having given up hope for this house, they received a call from the owner saying that he was now ready to accept their price.[55] The Craig family moved in and soon welcomed the church into their living room for relaxed and fairly informal worship services. Many who came were not used to such an informal house-church setting—David preached seated on the piano bench and, in the beginning, had to assure those gathered that the offerings were not going directly into his pockets![56] After several years the church, called *l'Église réformée St-Matthieu*, wanted a location that was more public and chose to move into a location on the campus of the University of Trois-Rivières.[57]

Church life in Trois-Rivières posed challenges not fully seen in Quebec. The church in Quebec had many young Christians eager to

---

54. Sermon 403.
55. Sermon 403.
56. Sermon 403.
57. Sermon 403. See also David's report to the Synod of the E.R.Q. (14 Mar. 1992). In this report he was very excited that the church now had a certain 'visibilité'. Several years later the church inquired about renting the St. James Anglican Church building, but it was voted down. See letter of D. Craig to St-James Anglican Church (6 Feb. 1991).

learn about evangelical Christianity and explore theology. In Trois-Rivières, however, many were by now in the workforce and had already been involved in other evangelical churches. More focus, then, was put on training and leading members of a Reformed church. Although it was not at first an issue, as the years passed David became more concerned about folks who were regular participants in the church, but did not want to become members. He tried to put more emphasis on what he considered to be the benefits of membership in a local church and the beauty of Reformed theology.

Besides some resistance to this call for membership, many did feel significant spiritual growth under David's ministry. One member noted that David's style of leadership was not imposing, but one which led by example. This member said that David would not try to convince his hearers of something simply by ordering it, but by persuading them to think the same thing by themselves. Hence, for this member David was not one to demand respect, but to merit it.

During these years at l'Église réformée St-Matthieu, David also found adverture outside the work at the church. For example, in 1985 David had the opportunity to visit Israel with a long-time friend, Daniel Racine. Racine was sent on behalf of an ecumenical centre in North America as a delegate to an ecumenical gathering in Jerusalem and brought David with him as an invited guest. David did not have much time to visit the many biblical sites, but he did appreciate being together with Christians from around the world. In fact, he knew a number of delegates from Western Europe because of his time in Switzerland in the early 1970s. As Daniel well knew, David loved to interact with other people, especially if the conversation happened around good wine and fine cheese!

CHAPTER NINE

United and Divided

WORKING TOGETHER?

While in Trois-Rivières David continued to build his contacts with other Reformed missionaries working with Francophones in Quebec. In fact, it was with the contacts gained in these cooperative Reformed works that the more clearly-defined goal of institutional unity was announced. At the request of the council of elders from the Reformed Church of the Beauce (which had affiliated itself with the more self-consciously evangelical Presbyterian Church in America and not The Presbyterian Church in Canada), the various Reformed churches involved in the Alliance Réformée Évangélique were encouraged to coordinate their missionary strategy and to gather together into one visible institution.[1] The Alliance had now more clearly defined its first objective of promoting unity as the forming of one united Reformed denomination in French Quebec. The variously affiliated congregations united informally in the Conseil des Églises

---

1. See "Rapport de la reunion des anciens et representants des églises groupements réformées au Québec," convoquée par les anciens de l'Église Catholique Réformée de St-George-de-Beauce, le 10 déc. 1983 à l'Église Réformée St-Marc de Ste-Foy. See also minutes of C.E.R.Q. (5 Jan. 1984).

Réformées du Québec (C.E.R.Q.) with the goal of formal union.

The goal of this Conseil was to have one French Reformed Church, but in full cooperation with The Presbyterian Church in Canada, the Presbyterian Church in America and the Christian Reformed Church. Many individuals in Quebec, including David, used as proof for this proposed union, the opinion of the French Canadian Missionary Society of the 19th century that such a unified ecclesiastical organism would be the most helpful for French Canadians.[2]

In February 1984 representatives from the three "mother" churches came together to discuss the future plans. The Christian Reformed Church and the Presbyterian Church in America representatives were enthusiastic, but The Presbyterian Church in Canada representatives, Ralph Kendall and Sam Priestly, were more cautious about the project. Both these men were very supportive of the goal of evangelisation, but reminded the other delegates that there were two French-speaking congregations in The Presbyterian Church in Canada (St-Paul in Melbourne and St-Luc in Montreal) that were not interested in joining this new denominational work. Hence, they argued, The Presbyterian Church in Canada needed to proceed with caution. Nonetheless, both were certainly open to coordinating mission projects better than the present situation.[3]

---

2. David frequently cited a master's dissertation of Richard Strout which stated that the vision of the Board of French Evangelization was to have one single voice in Quebec. David presented this vision before the Quebec Presbytery of The Presbyterian Church in Canada as evidence that the E.R.Q. was not entirely a foreign idea. Strout, Richard E. "The Latter Years of the Board of French Evangelization of the Presbyterian Church in Canada, 1895–1912," (M.A. thesis, Bishop's University, 1986), esp. 3–4, 11–12. See also the notes of his presentation on the work of the "Societé Missionnaire Canadienne-Française." Here he notes that the objectives of this organization were to share the gospel with French Canadians and that it desired to do this in as interdenominational a way as possible. "Societé Missionnaire Canadienne-Française," 3–4.

3. *Procès-verbal de la réunion du conseil des Églises réformées du Québec*

Despite the hesitancy of some in The Presbyterian Church in Canada, the plans for the future denomination went ahead. Several congregations had already become associate members of this future denomination in principle in the early summer of 1985. In the subsequent years, a church order was drawn up and confessional standards agreed upon (the Heidelberg Catechism and the Westminster Confession).[4] Several new pastors were examined by the C.E.R.Q. and installed as missionary pastors with one of the three "mother" churches.[5] The name of the new denomination was finally chosen: l'Église Réformée du Québec (E.R.Q.).[6]

As the structure and doctrine of the new denomination became better known, many, especially in The Presbyterian Church in Canada, needed to form a definite opinion for or against the proposed denomination. Healthy debates were had in a number of French and English publications concerning the viability of the new denomination. On the French side a number of pages were devoted to the question in the journal *La Vie Chrétienne* in 1986. In his opening article, Jean Porret underlined that the French-speaking Presbyterian churches were not all agreed on this issue. He wrote that he was concerned that the Église Réformée du Québec was involved with the Christian Reformed Church and the Presbyterian Church in America, but not with the United Church of Canada—which had genuine ties to the St-Luc Presbyterian Church in Montreal. He questioned the stance of this proposed Reformed denomination against the ordination of women to

---

avec les représentants des Églises-mères, tenue à Ste-Foy le 10 et 11 février, 1984, 4.

4. "Heidelberg" 6 November 1987 and "Westminster" 19 August 1988; Preliminary remarks for non-binding points of doctrine in the Westminster Confession were added: *Minutes of C.E.R.Q,* (19 Aug. 88): 7. The Heidelberg Catechism is one of the official confessions of Christian Reformed Church. The Westminster Confession is the official confession of The Presbyterian Church in America and The Presbyterian Church in Canada.

5. *Minutes of C.E.R.Q.* (6 Nov. 1987): 6.

6. *Minutes of C.E.R.Q.* (4 Mar. 1988): 6.

pastoral office.[7] In other articles, François Cordey and Paulin Bédard spoke on behalf the C.E.R.Q., Ralph Kendall for the Board of World Mission of The Presbyterian Church in Canada and Alison Patterson from her perspective at the St-Luc Church in Montreal.[8] These articles underline not only the great importance of working together, but also the various challenges to and models of common work.

The most pressing of these challenges was the disagreement over the promotion of and participation in the ordination of women to the office of elder and pastor in the church. It was true that in previous years, David had clearly made known his position on the issue of women's ordination. The Presbyterian Church in Canada had permitted the entry of women into the offices of pastor and ruling elder since 1966, but it was unclear what this meant for those who could not in good conscience participate in such an ordination. The issue was especially difficult for new pastoral candidates who did not agree with women's ordination. For this reason, in the late 1970s the General Assembly of the Presbyterian Church began to receive overtures on the subject and finally decided the issue in 1982. Some argued that those who permitted women's ordination to the office of pastor and elder and those who could not in good conscience agree with this permission, could still work together. Yet, the majority opinion adopted at the 1982 General Assembly was that any minister in The Presbyterian Church in Canada could enjoy an internal liberty of conscience, but not an external liberty of action (i.e. he could disagree with the ordination of women to the office of pastor and elder in his conscience, but had to participate in the ordination of a woman pastor or elder if called upon to do so).[9]

---

7. Jean Porret, "L'avenir des Franco-réformés? Un futur pas si clair," *La Vie Chrétienne* (Jan./Feb. 1986): 8.

8. *La Vie Chrétienne* (Jan./Feb. 1986): 8–11.

9. For one account of this Assembly and the struggle over this issue see: K.J. Stewart, "Conscience controversy dominates Presbyterian Assembly," *Calvinist Contact* (9 Jul. 1982).

The decision had very practical implications for David and those who supported him. In January 1982 the Côte-des-Neiges Presbyterian Church in Montreal had called John Vaudry to be their pastor. Vaudry had studied at The Presbyterian College in Montreal and was at the time sent out as a pastor to Cape Breton Island by the Board of World Mission. He was ordained several years previous in Sherbrooke by the Presbytery of Quebec—the Rev. David Craig officiating. Hence, when in February 1982 the Presbytery of Montreal did not sustain Vaudry's call because of his unwillingness to participate in the ordination of women to the office of elder and pastor, David was quite taken aback.[10] Further, with the decision of the General Assembly in June 1982 basically confirming the actions of the Presbytery of Montreal, David felt compelled to register his disapproval.

David's position at this point was not that The Presbyterian Church in Canada should immediately eliminate all women ministers and elders (although he personally did not find a biblical precedent for such ordinations, he had lived with women being ordained in the same denomination for his whole Presbyterian career), but that the Presbyterian Church could not *force* those who disagreed to participate in these ordinations. So, in November 1982 David drafted a letter signed by the members of the St-Marc Church which strenuously disagreed with this "liberty of conscience, but not of action" barrier laid on new pastors. The letter basically argued that this 'barrier act' was unbiblical and unpresbyterian. To disjoin conscience and action, argued David and his parishioners, was fundamentally wrong. [11]

---

10. A short history of this question in The Presbyterian Church in Canada is found in Moir, *Enduring Witness*, 280–82. For more detail on this incident and Vaudry's perspective see: John Vaudry, *Built on the Rock: A History of Cote des Neiges Presbyterian Church, Montreal* (Montreal: 2008), 55–62.

11. In the letter David and his congregation members note they are not in agreement with the decision concerning women's ordination by which even ordained and inducted ministers in the Presbyterian church could have 'freedom of belief but not action' as reflected in the 108th General Assembly's decision relating to Book of Forms 407:4. The letter (written by David, but

As noted, the 'barrier act' had a practical impact on many English-speaking congregations across Canada, but, one could argue, especially on the various French congregations in the Presbytery of Quebec. Several candidates for the ministry who presented themselves for French work in that Presbytery beside David held a similar position and could not in good conscience agree to the greater restrictions imposed by the 1982 General Assembly. David helped present before Presbytery candidates like François Cordey for ordination, but soon found it impossible, for new candidates no longer had the limited liberty that David still enjoyed (David was ordained and had not yet been asked to participate in an ordination ceremony of a women elder or pastor).[12] The ordination of women to the office of pastor and elder, then, came

---

endorsed by the members and adherents of the Église St-Marc), makes this statement: "We contend that there has been a basic, fundamental alteration in doctrine (without benefit of the Barrier Act) in declaring that teaching and ruling elders are responsible to the church rather than to Christ in the first instance. This coupled with the fact that there is no longer 'freedom of action' regarding the ordination of women shows that we have elevated the church above Jesus-Christ. The principle of liberty of conscience and responsibility to our Lord, established in our courts by our Reformation Fathers, Luther, Calvin and Knox, is now extinct, and with it our legitimacy as a church founded upon and agreeable to the Word of God." Members and adherents of the Église St-Marc, "Letter to Presbytery of Quebec," (9 Nov. 1982). Several years later (and now as pastor in the newly-formed E.R.Q.) David wrote a short unpublished document entitled 'le rôle feminin' in which he presented further reflection and arguments. This was prepared for the April meeting of the 'comité du ministère' of the E.R.Q. In reflecting on his previous experience in The Presbyterian Church in Canada, he remarked that he was principally disappointed by his perception that The Presbyterian Church in Canada went ahead with the ordination of women based on pragmatic reasons and not close biblical study.

12. François Cordey was finally ordained in the E.R.Q. on 17 September 1989. David preached the sermon for the occasion noting that François was one of the first graduates of the Institut Farel and that he was now being ordained in the E.R.Q., a denomination which was the work of the Spirit of God. Sermon 793.

to the fore as the critical dividing line between the C.E.R.Q. and The Presbyterian Church in Canada.

David's evangelical colleagues in Quebec and across Canada knew that David found no biblical warrant to accept the ordination of women as pastors and elders, but they could still work informally together even if they disagreed on the matter. Further, ever since his university days he had encountered differences with others in the denomination. David considered himself generally an evangelical in The Presbyterian Church in Canada (he wholeheartedly supported the foundation of The Renewal Fellowship within The Presbyterian Church in Canada) and took exception to many of his colleagues' "liberal" tendencies. However, the controversy on the "barrier act" of 1982 and the division over the E.R.Q. was different, but not simply because it caused division. It was different because this controversy forcibly separated him not only from his 'liberal' colleagues, but now also from many close colleagues on the 'evangelical' side of The Presbyterian Church in Canada. The decisions of the General Assembly of June 1982, then, had direct implications in the unwillingness of the Presbyterian Church in Canada to support the formation of the E.R.Q. in the years following.

There was a second issue, however, which also caused many within The Presbyterian Church in Canada to be cautious about the E.R.Q. One could argue that David's proposition was also hampered by lingering bitterness about the 'divisive' actions of many in the founding of the United Church in Canada in 1925. One might argue that one of the great unpardonable crimes of The Presbyterian Church in Canada after 1925 was causing any sort of division. Not only was the E.R.Q., in the minds of many, causing division, but it was also in close contact with the Presbyterian Church in America which had only relatively recently (in the early 1970s) divided from the Presbyterian Church (USA).[13] Consequently, many in The Presbyterian Church in Canada

---

13. On the history and theology of the Presbyterian Church in America see: Sean Lucas, *On Being Presbyterian: Our Beliefs, Practices, and Stories* (Phillipsburg, New Jersey: P&R Publishing, 2006).

were wary of such division and could not support what they saw as a competing denomination in the same country.

SEPARATION OR UNION?

In the summer of 1988 the General Assembly of The Presbyterian Church in Canada started to speak more clearly about its relationship to the proposed E.R.Q. David had proposed that he be 'seconded' to the E.R.Q. so he could work with the group but still officially be a Presbyterian. The proposal was difficult, for some asked whether they could support the 'seconding' of individual missionaries like David without supporting the E.R.Q. denomination as such. Many in The Presbyterian Church in Canada had great respect for David, but a growing number, for reasons cited above, did not want to officially support the E.R.Q.[14]

At the General Assembly a special committee was formed to examine the question. Important in the report by this committee was the unity of the Presbyterian church in all parts of Canada and that because of its "reformed polity" it was unable to give congregations the possibility of withdrawing.[15] The recommendations that were adopted then wanted to promote the work of mission in Quebec, but not to support officially the new denomination.[16] When the Rev. J.H. Kouwenberg moved David's idea that The Presbyterian Church in Canada ought to 'second' its pastors and workers wishing to participate in the *Église Réformée du Québec*, the motion was referred to the Committee on Ecumenical Relations.[17] From these discussions at the level of General Assembly, one begins to see the official dividing line being drawn more clearly.

---

14. *Acts and Proceedings of General Assembly* (1988): 463-468. See also Tom Kurdyla (delegate of Montreal), "114e Assemblé générale de l'Église presbytérienne au Canada et ministère francophone," *La Vie Chrétienne* (Jul./Aug. 1988): 12.

15. *Acts and Proceedings of General Assembly* (1988): 468.

16. *Acts and Proceedings of General Assembly* (1988): 30–31, 468.

17. *Acts and Proceedings of General Assembly* (1988): 31.

One can better understand David's reasoning at this critical juncture in an interview in *Channels* magazine in 1988.[18] *Channels* was a venture of The Renewal Fellowship within The Presbyterian Church in Canada, an organization committed to renewing spiritual vitality and historic biblical witness in and through The Presbyterian Church in Canada.[19] Indeed, David had many theological and personal friends among those involved in this fellowship. More, for more than a decade David had received significant moral and financial help from this group. It was only natural, then, that David be asked his opinion on the proposed French Reformed denomination on the horizon. To put the interview in perspective, the editors of *Channels* preceded it with a page of quoted text from the report of the Special Committee examining the proposed French Reformed denomination included in the minutes of the 114th General Assembly.[20]

We see some of the chagrin David experienced facing this unpleasant defeat in this interview. In the interview David reiterated his opinion that a unified E.R.Q. was not a new idea in the Presbyterian Church, but was the same mission held by the French Canadian Missionary Society of the 19th century. Second, he expressed regret over the General Assembly's apparent 'no' to the E.R.Q. during their meeting in June of that year. He knew that a major stumbling block in the

---

18. "An Interview with David Craig." *Channels* 5/3-4 (Summer/Fall 1988): 15–17.

19. See A. Donald MacLeod, "Looking Back Over Twenty Years of *Channels*," *Channels* 19/1 (Spring 2003). MacLeod makes specific comments about David and the breakup with the Presbyterian church: "Indigenous Francophone work within the Presbyterian Church in Canada, encouraged by the Fellowship, seemed so promising in those early years. In a 1988 *Channels* interview David Craig stated: 'We are dealing with a grass-roots situation; these are Quebecois and it is French people doing French work and not a French work being thrust upon them from the outside.' Alas, a middle way could not be found: as a church we lost any claim to be a church bringing together the two solitudes of our founding nations."

20. See *Acts and Proceedings of General Assembly* (1988): 463–468.

relationship between the two was the issue of women's ordination. He made it clear that he would join the E.R.Q., but still wished to have his credentials recognized in The Presbyterian Church in Canada and be supported financially and in prayer in his work by like-minded congregations and individuals in the church.[21] David's interview was followed up by an article by Hans Kouwenberg who moved the motion at the 114th Assembly to 'second' The Presbyterian Church in Canada missionaries to the Reformed Church of Quebec. Although the motion was defeated, Kouwenberg again made the plea for flexibility when dealing with such mission projects, especially when dealing with mission projects in places like Quebec where the Presbyterian church does not have a strong presence.[22]

Because the lines were being more clearly drawn, much heated debate ensued at the September meeting of the Presbytery of Quebec. It was proposed by David and those supporting the E.R.Q. that the Presbytery go ahead and support the 'seconding' of individual applicants to the almost-inaugurated denomination even though the matter had not yet been finally settled by the General Assembly (it was being considered by the Ecumenical Relations committee).[23] Therefore, an amendment was added to the proposal that would make the "seconding" subject to the approval of the 115th General Assembly in 1989. Some wanted to add an amendment to the amendment, but the proposal itself was narrowly defeated.[24] Although he voted against the proposal, one of the presbyters, the Rev. Blake Walker, went on record saying that his vote was against the proposal and not against David's person or his calibre as a pastor.[25] Additionally, the Presbytery ruled against the desire of

---

21. "An Interview with David Craig." *Channels* 5/3–4 (Summer/Fall 1988): 15–17.

22. J.H. (Hans) Kouwenberg, "The Reformed Church of Quebec: l'Église Réformée du Québec," *Channels* 5/3–4 (Summer/Fall 1988): 18-19.

23. Minutes, *The Presbytery of Quebec* (15 Sept. 1988): 712.

24. Minutes, *The Presbytery of Quebec* (15 Sept. 1988): 713.

25. "The Rev. Blake Walker asked to have the following statement

St-Marc Church in Quebec to withdraw from The Presbyterian Church in Canada to join the E.R.Q.[26]

One detail at the end of the discussion concerning the Francophone work which would greatly impact David's life was the reworking of the Francophone Committee of Presbytery.[27] The original recommendation read as follows:

> That the Presbytery of Quebec discharge the present members of the Francophone Committee with thanks; that the Presbytery of Quebec dissolve the Trois-Rivières Area Committee, that the responsibility for French work be placed with the Sherbrooke Area Committee.[28]

However, two presbyters, Lyle Sams and Blake Walker amended this recommendation to replace the last sentence of the recommendation, "... that the responsibility for French work ... " with "... that a Francophone Committee with direct reporting to Presbytery be established with the Rev. Daniel Forget as convener."[29] This new committee, purged, one could say, of those friendly to the cause of the E.R.Q. and with the Rev. Forget as convenor, would prove decisive in David's exclusion from The Presbyterian Church in Canada.

Rev. Forget is of special importance. He had only *very* recently become part of the Presbytery of Quebec after being pastor of a Pentecostal church for some time. He was in large part in the Presbyterian church on the recommendation of David, whom he had gotten to know

---

recorded in the minutes: 'In view of some suggestions coming out of the discussion just held, I wish it recorded that my vote against seconding Mr. Craig and Mr. Davidson to the proposed Église Reformee du Quebec is in no way to be construed as withholding recognition of the high calibre of their personal faith and dedication, of their pastoral and evangelistic leadership.'" Minutes, *The Presbytery of* Quebec (15 Sept. 1988): 714.

26. Minutes, *The Presbytery of Quebec* (15 Sept. 1988): 714.
27. Minutes, *The Presbytery of Quebec* (15 Sept. 1988): 715.
28. Minutes, *The Presbytery of Quebec* (15 Sept. 1988): 715.
29. Minutes, *The Presbytery of Quebec* (15 Sept. 1988): 715.

in Trois-Rivières. Rev. Forget had studied in the department of theology of the University of Trois-Rivières and received a master's degree from the department in 1989.[30]

In fact, it was in June 1988 that he was 'received' as pastor of St-Paul's Church in Melbourne—a service at which Rev. Walker gave the blessing.[31] At Rev. Forget's installation it was assumed that he would complete his study of Canadian church history and Presbyterian Church government as had previously been asked of him. Under the tutelage of David and Rev. Walker, he was assigned to read approximately sixteen works on Presbyterian history, Reformed theology and Presbyterian church government over the summer of 1988. He was then given a general exam by a representative of Presbytery on 1 September 1988.[32] It was only at this point that he could be officially installed as pastor of St-Paul's Church in Melbourne.

Although Rev. Forget was not trained as a Presbyterian pastor and was still very new to the Presbyterian situation, his importance resided in the fact that he was a *real* Quebecois, and, as such, was understood by some to represent what Francophones *really* wanted. Perhaps this led to his rapid rise to lead the Francophone Committee and Francophone work of the Presbyterian Church. In October 1988 Forget

---

30. Daniel H. Forget, "Une réflexion en église sur les attitudes et les comportements chrétiens face aux situations conflictuelles de l'agir humain." (M.A. thesis, Université de Québec à Trois-Rivières, 1989).

31. See minutes, *The Presbytery of Quebec* (16 Jun. 1988): 703.

32. Presbyterian History—*Enduring Witness, Resistance to Church Union in Canada*, "The French Canadian Missionary Society" (thesis) and *Chiniquy*. Doctrine and Practice—"Historical digest of the work in Articles of Faith" 1942-67, *Confession et Catechisme de Westminster, The Westminster Assembly and its Work* (John Leith), *Systematic Theology* (L. Berkoff) and *Homme et Femme dans la Morale Calvinienne*. Operation and management – *The Book of Forms*, "Questions vis-à-vis le Book of Forms," *Foi Vivante, Social Action Handbook, The Eldership in Today's Church, Guidebook for Church Managment* and the "Declaratory Act of 1980". See minutes, *The Presbytery of Quebec* (17 Nov. 1988): 743.

was already asked to lead a "Strategic Planning Seminar" for a special meeting of Presbytery.[33] By December 1988 Forget was proposed as part-time coordinator of Francophone ministries.[34]

It is important to understand the difference in the mission vision of Rev. Forget and David Craig. Rev. Forget's vision for Francophone ministry in the Presbyterian church can be gleaned indirectly from a committee as a report to the General Assembly in June 1990 on French evangelisation[35] and directly in an article submitted in French to *La Vie Chrétienne* in 1990 and, two years later, to *The Presbyterian Record*.[36]

The report begins noting that the 114th General Assembly clearly stipulated that Francophone work had to be done within The Presbyterian Church in Canada and not under the auspices of the Église réformée du Québec. This stated, the goal of the report was to gain new clarity and momentum for French work within the Presbyterian Church. First, the committee outlined a history of French work. In its opinion the most successful point was under the Board of French Evangelisation in the 19th century. The less successful moments occurred during the tenure of certain "personalities" who gave a boost to French work, but were only temporarily successful or led to division. The most natural way of reading this report is to understand David as one of these "personalities". The committee noticed that David had aroused intrest in French work and attracted a certain number of young men to

---

33. Minutes of meeting *pro re nata*, *The Presbytery of Quebec* (27 Oct. 1988): 719.

34. Minutes of meeting *pro re nata*, *The Presbytery of Quebec* (12 Dec. 1988): 767–68.

35. Ministère francophone, consistoire du Québec [Daniel Forget, executive secretary], "Rapport du Comité spécial sur la stratégie du Ministère francophone," 4 pp. [Archives of the Presbytery of Montreal at The Presbyterian College, "Église présbyterienne St-Luc, Ministère francophone, 1986–90."]

36. Daniel Forget, "L'option presbytérienne: Une continuité historique, un choix d'avenir," *La Vie Chrétienne* (Avril-Mai 1990): 8–9; and "The Presbyterian Option: a Historical Continuity, a Choice for the Future," *The Presbyterian Record* (Jan. 1992): 32-33.

the ministry, but many of these men "decided to join" other denominations like The Presbyterian Church in America and, eventually, the Église réformée du Québec. The committee expressed confidence that despite this departure there were still an increasing number of francocanadian leaders ready to found and lead "faith communities" within The Presbyterian Church in Canada. These leaders, says the report, "would have a high intellectual standard, but also be well rooted in daily life." Further, the report reminds The Presbyterian Church in Canada that "the time is ripe for The Presbyterian Church in Canada to offer an alternative, a ministry which addresses all aspects of the human person."[37] The report ends by recommending the formation of a new national committee of francophone ministry. This national committee could oversee all the French-language work of the Presbyterian Church in Canada.

Five things should be noted about this report which contrast Forget's vision with that of David Craig. First, it is assumed that the arguments given against the E.R.Q. at the 114th General Assembly are correct—especially the argument that the E.R.Q. is, in fact, not a work of The Presbyterian Church in Canada. Second, the history of the work of French evangelisation given in the report does not well represent the historical and cultural situation in which the Board of French Evangelization was formed in the 19th century. The success of French evangelisation in the 19th century can be linked to many other factors than simply the presence of a Board of French Evangelisation.[38] Next, the use of such terms as "personalities" to refer to key figures in 20th century French evangelisation is clearly pejorative and minimizes these men's positive impact and committment to The Presbyterian Church in Canada. Fourthly, several men influenced by David and wanting to present themselves for ordination in The Presbyterian Church in

---

37. "Le temps est propice à ce que l'Eglise presbytèrienne au Canada offre une alternative, un ministère s'adressant à toutes les facettes de l'être humain." Ministère francophone, "Rapport," (1989), 3.

38. For example, see Lalonde, *Des Loups dans la bergerie*, 222–263.

Canada were rejected by it before they "decided to join" other denominations. Finally, the committee's positive vision for the work of French evangelisation is not clear. For example, the committee argues that the time is ripe for an "alternative" kind of ministry—an alternative to what? The answer is far from apparent. One option is that a new type of ministry ought to be developed under a national committee of francophone ministry which seeks a sort of unity and holism, not like the divisive and "personality"-driven work of previous evangelists like David Craig.

Forget wrote the committee report, presumably, with others, but he also penned his own article for *La vie chrétienne* and, later, translated in the *Presbyterian Record*. This article reproduced important points from the committee report, but was now from Forget personally and concerned the E.R.Q. specifically. The argument of the article is often elusive to the reader, but the conclusion is clear enough—Forget did not agree with the theology and vision of David Craig or the E.R.Q.[39] In particular, Rev. Forget argued that the E.R.Q. somehow would "deculturize" French Canadians, which was poor missionary strategy in his opinion.[40] The article does not make it specific, but *somehow*

---

39. "Who are the supporters of this new denomination, the Reform Church of Québec? They are people who identify with Calvinism and aim at restoring the place of the New Testament and the Reformed tradition in the hearts of the Québécois people. They interpret the Holy Scriptures literally, sometimes applying them more rigorously than at other times. Their deductive and rather exclusive theological approach seeks to create a homogeneous group reflecting pure doctrine. This cuts across the diversity of ideology and theological pluralism in which we live. Values in such an environment, values of both religious beliefs and social ethics, tend to be uniform and standardized (a pressuring status quo) in order to maintain this homogeneity." Forget, "The Presbyterian Option," 32.

40. "I do not believe that the transmission of faith of the Presbyterian or Reformed tradition should be done at the price of deculturalizing Franco-Canadians, causing them to lose their identity as a people with their own culture and history. The distinctive characters of the two founding peoples of our country should be preserved in a union where both are respectful." Forget,

being in The Presbyterian Church in Canada lets the Quebecois still be Quebecois—in some indescribable way a Francophone is more free in the Presbyterian Church than in the E.R.Q.[41] Nowhere does Rev. Forget speak of the technicalities of 'seconding' or of church polity, but rather always comes back to the perceived doctrinal rigidity of the E.R.Q. This is telling, for his problem is not the E.R.Q. as such, but the confessional and evangelical doctrine of the denomination. Somehow the Presbyterian church was in touch with "reality" in a way in which the E.R.Q. was not.[42] Forget's opposition to the E.R.Q., then, was quite different from that of Rev. Walker who had opposed it more clearly on the basis of church order and not on evangelical doctrine. In fact, as Rev. Walker noted publicly, he had always had great respect for David as a person and a colleague.[43]

A FEW MOMENTOUS MONTHS

Several other meetings in late September and October 1988 continued to deepen the divide. On 23 September the Synodical Committee on Francophone Ministry met in St. Andrew's Church in Sherbrooke to discuss general matters, but particularly the developments at St-Marc Church and in Trois-Rivières. For reasons unknown, David, who was

---

"The Presbyterian Option," 33.

41. "Apostolic teaching originated in a different culture, age and society from our own. It is the responsibility of men and women of every age to reformulate their faith in God in the cultural context in which they live. In executing this reformulation of faith, we should be careful not to obscure the basic message behind various forms of expression that were the result of personal experience or journeys. The Holy Scriptures are not to be treated as simply another work of literature. At the same time, we must be careful not to impose a culture or a human tradition on another." Forget, "The Presbyterian Option," 33.

42. "The present demands productivity, practicality and the proclamation of the gospel adapted to contemporary and Canadian realities." Forget, "The Presbyterian Option," 33.

43. Minutes, *The Presbytery of Quebec* (15 Sept. 1988): 714.

UNITED AND DIVIDED

supposed to be moderator, could not make the meeting. Two invited guests, however, did come—Ian Morrison of the Board of World Mission and Rev. Walker, minister in Sherbrooke.[44] Both Morrison and Rev. Walker had a keen interest in seeing that the matter with David and the E.R.Q. be resolved quickly.

This interest was again evidenced on 27 October when the Presbytery had a special (*Pro re nata*) meeting to discuss the impending inauguration of the E.R.Q.[45] David was present at this meeting, but seemed resolute in his interest to be sent to the new denomination and all the while to stay a faithful Presbyterian minister. One senses the frustration of the other delegates at this meeting even in written documents, but little could be done at this point to stop the lines being drawn.

As expected, David and the church at Trois-Rivières joined with the E.R.Q. at its inauguration on 6 November 1988 in a ceremony at the Château Frontenac in Québec City.[46] Nancy and David described the event in their annual letter to friends:

> November 6, 1988 was a memorable day for all of us. The Eglise Réformée du Québec was born in a beautiful, joyful ceremony at the historic Château Frontenac in Quebec City. There were about 400 present, including guests from other denominations and from the 'mother Churches.' (The Presbyterian Church in Canada was invited but no one came.) As the assembly rose to sing Handel's 'A Toi la Gloire', accompanied by a brass trumpet, there were many tears of

---

44. Minutes, *Synod Committee: Francophone Ministry, sub-committee of Canada Operations* (23 Sept. 1988): 1.
45. Minutes of meeting *pro re nata*, *The Presbytery of Quebec* (27 Oct. 1988): 718–720.
46. The formation of this denomination even made it into the press: "L'Église réformée du Québec s'etablit officiellement," *Le Soleil* [Quebec], (samedi 5 Nov. 1988); "Une 'sorte de schisme' chez les presbytériens," *La Presse* (6 Nov. 1988): B5; Harvey Shepherd, "New French Reform church established," *The Gazette* [Montreal], (Sat, 12 Nov. 1988): K9; *Christian Observer* (28 Oct. 1988): 11; *Aujourd'hui Credo* 35/9 (Nov. 1988): 15; Harold Jantz, "New church out of old roots," *Christian Week* (25 Oct. 1988): 2.

joy. The dream of more than 128 years had become a reality. As the people of Israel by faith put their feet into the Jordan and waited for God to open the river miraculously, so the assembled group took their step of faith and are looking forward to watching their faithful God perform miracles![47]

For this occasion David worked together with Paulin Bédard to draw up a theological and historical introduction to the newly-formed denomination.[48] David also worked a great deal on the further revision of the "Ordre et discipline ecclésiastique" during the early years of the denomination.

David's joining officially with the E.R.Q. before the matter was settled in The Presbyterian Church in Canada was opposed by a number of his Presbyterian colleagues. This issue came to a head at the November meeting of the Presbytery of Quebec. The tone was set early for the rest of the meeting's outcome. A certain adherent of the St-Matthieu Church wrote a letter to Presbytery giving his perspective on the E.R.Q., encouraging them to support this new experiment. Several delegates pointed out that the letter seemed to confuse the E.R.Q. with the previous C.E.R.Q. Hence, the Rev. David Kettle, supported by Daniel Forget, proposed that a letter be sent to this gentleman informing him:

> [T]hat the P.C.C. has always been willing to cooperate with a loose federation of reformed congregations (such as C.E.R.Q.) but stops short of supporting a new denomination (E.R.Q.). It is our conten-

---

47. Letter to friends (Apr. 1989): 2.
48. *Église Réformée du Québec*, the verso of the first page explains that this 35 page text was "written by David Craig and Paulin Bédard at the behest of the committee preparing the inauguration of the *Église réformée du Québec*. It is with joy that this booklet is presented at this memorable to the members, colleagues and friends of the E.R.Q. Quebec, 6 November 1988" [translation mine]. The text includes a brief summary of the history, beliefs, structure and goals of the new denomination. Pages 34 and 35 list church activities in 11 regions.

tion that the P.C.C. has operated an effective francophone ministry in Quebec in the past, continues to do so at the present moment, and will continue to do so until Christ call us all home.[49]

Implicit in this response is the nub of the question. Many delegates simply could not accept that the work of David in the E.R.Q. ought to still be considered the work of The Presbyterian Church in Canada. From David's perspective this was precisely the problem—these delegates were putting the present institution of The Presbyterian Church of Canada above the progress of mission in Quebec. David's contention was that the E.R.Q. *was* The Presbyterian Church in Canada's mission and that it could continue to be so. Whether it was because of the E.R.Q.'s more confessional theology, their stance against the ordination of women elders and pastors, or even the lack of the word 'Presbyterian' in their name, it was now a matter of choice. For many the choice was simple: either one was with The Presbyterian Church in Canada or not—no more compromise was possible.

It seemed logical, then, for some delegates to propose that all workers sign an oath of loyalty to The Presbyterian Church in Canada. This oath was proposed by the Francophone Committee now composed of Mr. Pierre Desveaux, Mr. Scott Emery (secretary), Rev. Blake Walker and Rev. Daniel Forget (convenor). Previously on 2 October, there had been a meeting at St. Andrew's Presbyterian in Sherbrooke to ask an oath of loyalty to the Presbyterian Church specifically from Patrice Michaud. Michaud, an evangelist with St. Andrew's in Sherbrooke in francophone ministry for the previous year, had affinities with the project of the E.R.Q. and, hence, was not willing to sign the loyalty oath.[50] The matter was taken up again on 17 November at the full meeting of the Presbytery in Valcartier Village mentioned above.[51]

---

49. Minutes, *The Presbytery of Quebec* (17 Nov. 1988): 726.
50. See minutes, *The Presbytery of Quebec* (17 Nov. 1988): 738.
51. Minutes, *The Presbytery of Quebec* (17 Nov. 1988): 736, 750.

At this meeting the Francophone Committee made clear their understanding of loyalty to the Presbyterian Church (here quoted in its complete form):

> Given that the 114th General Assembly of our church has approved the report of the Special Committee re: Eglise Réformée du Québec, while at the same time accepting the recommendation that the matter of seconding pastors and workers to the new denomination be referred to the Ecumenical Relations Committee, we now find ourselves in a delicate and possibly confusing situation concerning the oversight of our Francophone ministry. Our responsibility is to ensure that there be no conflict or lack of harmony in ministry during the months leading to the 115th General Assembly in June 1989. Recent events have shown that divisive acts have already taken place. The following recommendation is offered in a prayerful spirit, with the desire that it will assist all members of Presbytery and workers, to work together in the unity of Christ:
>
> Whereas, the 114th General Assembly of the Presbyterian Church in Canada approved the report of the Special Committee on Overture #35 Cf. l'Eglise Réformée du Québec, and Whereas, the Presbytery of Quebec cannot encourage a schismatic Spirit or permit a divisive course under the pretext of ecumenism, and . . . " Motion: (Kettle/Forget) That the phrase commencing with Whereas and ending with ecumenism be removed. Carried. Whereas, the Presbytery cannot shirk its responsibility as a corporate bishop, and Whereas, the Francophone Committee has been approached by a considerable number of Presbyters and other Elders who are deeply concerned about the length of time given to French work in the Presbytery without resolution of the recurring tensions and divisions, over the past several years, Therefore be it recommended:
>
> Recommendation: (Walker/Emery) That all workers of the Francophone work of the Presbytery of Quebec sign the following declaration:

"By this present, I certify having the intention and desire to work loyally for the Presbyterian Church in Canada in support of the Francophone ministry under the oversight of the Presbytery of Quebec. I declare that I will not participate in the organization of the new denomination, l'Eglise Réformée du Québec, that I will not promote E.R.Q. among my parishioners, and that I will not solicit members for this new denomination.

"The refusal to sign this declaration will be understood as a contrary stance. Such individuals would bring upon themselves the discipline of the Presbytery leading to their removal from their positions." Carried[52]

Several delegates, including David, immediately objected to such an oath. David considered it *ultra vires*, meaning that the Presbytery was claiming more power than it actually had. Nonetheless, the Presbytery continued with its business and asked all members to respond to the oath. Of the nineteen people asked, three could not in good conscience respond in the affirmative: David, Patrice Michaud and Ross Davidson. David mentioned that he was appealing this motion to a higher church body, Patrice and Ross were deemed to have implicitly said 'no'.[53]

In his appeal, David claimed such an oath was based on a faulty definition of "loyalty" contained in the oath. Further, he claimed that this oath and its threats without *specific* charges of wrongdoing being laid, was against the rules on judicial process in The Presbyterian Church in Canada's *Book of Forms*.[54] He was allowed to produce an appeal for the following synod meeting, but his appeal was not accepted on several

---

52. Minutes, *The Presbytery of Quebec* (17 Nov. 1988): 735–736.
53. Minutes, *The Presbytery of Quebec* (18 Nov. 1988): 750–751.
54. In his appeal and complaint to the 1989 General Assembly David cites the current *Book of Forms* sections 316 and 316.1 as evidence for his case.

grounds.⁵⁵ The result was that at the level of Presbytery David no longer had room to move.⁵⁶

David's last hope was the report of the Ecumenical Relations Committee to the 1989 General Assembly on the matter of 'seconding' ministers to the Reformed Church of Quebec. His hope was that the General Assembly would be more willing to 'second' than was the Presbytery of Quebec. The Ecumenical Relations Committee examined the issue, but noted that the sort of 'seconding' proposed was not appropriate, for it would introduce another denomination into a geographical region where The Presbyterian Church in Canada already had missionaries doing similar work. Indeed, the Board of World Mission of The Presbyterian Church in Canada had entered into 'seconding' arrangements abroad where The Presbyterian Church in Canada had no base of operations, but in Quebec this was not the case. They reiterated their support and encouragement of ministry among Francophones, but not by way of 'seconding' ministers.⁵⁷ Nonetheless, one delegate moved an amendment to support for two more years missionaries in the E.R.Q. where there was no Francophone Presbyterian Church, but this amendment was defeated.⁵⁸

AFTER THE STORM

If the events that occurred in Nigeria were the most intense of David's life, the events surrounding the break-up of his relationship with The Presbyterian Church in Canada were the most heart-breaking. The issue was so difficult for David (and for many of those involved) because close colleagues and friends had to take a stand on opposite sides. Indeed, David was profoundly disappointed with colleagues who "turned against him" after more than a decade of common work. The

---

55. *Minutes of Presbytery of Quebec* (16 Feb. 1989): 777.
56. Some of the final fallout is seen in the *Minutes of Synod of Quebec and Eastern Ontario* (1992): 5, 16 and Appendix 8.1.
57. *Acts and Proceedings of General Assembly* (1989); 27–28, 361–62.
58. *Acts and Proceedings of General Assembly* (1989): 28.

rupture of his relationship with the church was a sour pill to swallow—especially because he felt (rightly or wrongly) that many of those who ought to have supported him did not. Besides the specific question of the legitimacy of the E.R.Q., David was extremely saddened to see that many in The Presbyterian Church in Canada had more in common with a kind of pluralist and non-confessional vision for Francophone ministry like that of Daniel Forget than with his.

The details of this sad episode are still somewhat misunderstood or misrepresented in subsequent history of The Presbyterian Church in Canada and *Église Réformée du Québec*. For example, in his otherwise fine study on the history of The Presbyterian Church in Canada, John Moir gives scant and unbalanced attention to these difficult events in statements on "unity and diversity":

> This increased involvement of women in all aspects of the Church's life and mission seemed symbolic of a spirit of optimism and a catholicity of outlook growing in the Church as the last decade before the millennium was approached, even though some major problems remained unresolved including the widening gap between the evangelical and 'liberal' groups in the church. In 1990 evangelical Francophone congregations separated to establish their own small but determined church, L'Église Réformée de Québec, but for the majority of evangelicals the watchword for the future was given by the Rev. Mariano DiGangi who reminded them that, 'Renewal of the Presbyterian Church in Canada must be our concern, not its disruption.'[59]

Despite giving the wrong date and name, Moir is not careful with his description of the reasoning behind the foundation of the Eglise Réformée *du* Québec in 1988. Indeed, David argued strenuously that such a foundation was not a 'separation' nor was it his 'own' work.[60]

---

59. Moir, *Enduring Witness*, 293.
60. See sermons E92 and E96. See also David's article "450 ans d'Histoire et une bougie pour les Eglises Réformées du Québec," *Le Christianisme au XXe siècle* 231 (4 Nov. 1989): 8-9. David's article gives a survey of the work in

Rather, he wanted the new denomination to be a union of sorts of the work of the various Reformed missionaries and, indeed, considered as the Presbyterian Church's *own* work.[61] The split severed many of David's relationships with those in the church and was a source of disappointment for the rest of his life.[62] Nonetheless, he was still content

---

Quebec essentially similar to that published a year earlier with Paulin Bédard at the inauguration ceremony of the E.R.Q. The argument is that the E.R.Q. is essentially the same work that had been begun by The Presbyterian Church in Canada. In a subsequent number of the same magazine, Gérard Gautier, director of *Aujourd'hui Credo* and member of the United Church of Canada, wrote a letter to the editor in response arguing the opposite. Gautier thanks David for his enthusiastic article, but deplores the fact that David did not mention the work of the Francophone work of the Presbyterian Church in Canada and the United Church in Canada in the region of Montreal. Gautier considers that David has presumed a monopoly on "Reformed" work in Quebec. Further, Gautier notes that the E.R.Q. was supposed to resolve questions of division, but it simply separated into anther French denomination. Finally, the vision of the E.R.Q. (first seen in the "Manifeste de Montmorency") was far too conservative, especially in its decision against the ordination of women to the office of pastor and elder and its rejection of all theologicial pluralism. Gérard Gautier, "Les Protestants du Canada," *Le Christianisme au XXe siècle* [232?]: 4.

61. Owing to the heat and hurt of the debate, David sometimes overstepped his boundaries. In sermon 506 on 30 July 1989, he likened the Presbytery's forcing of the French churches to remain in The Presbyterian Church in Canada to the judaizing Christians of Acts 11 forcing the Gentiles to live as Jews. David argues that a gentile Christian dominated by the Judaizers is equal to a Quebecois dominated by Anglophone Presbyterians. This dangerous analogy is characteristic of the intense pain David felt about Presbytery immediately after the turmoil of 1988–89. This analogy was not characteristic of his argument before the issue came to a head.

62. See sermon 797 and E92. Also, In the small article "L'E.R.Q. à cinq ans," David reiterated his opinion that the ERQ was the true inheritor of the French Canadian Missionary Society of the 19th century whose goal was to have one unified French Reformed mission. In this article we see that David was still somewhat upset about what he perceived as denominationalism on the part of The Presbyterian Church in Canada: "Two *mother* churches accepted the changes with enthusiasm and adopted the principle that the C.E.R.Q. would be their *arm* in Quebec. The C.E.R.Q. would be their *mission*

with his decision to join the E.R.Q. and considered its formation a work of the Lord.[63]

---

in the province and they would no longer establish francophone churches from their own denomination. An agreement made this decision official and was signed by the Christian Reformed Church and The Presbyterian Church in America. But The Presbyterian Church in Canada, even though it agreed in principle with the formation of a francophone Church, became hesitant. Citing its doctrinal latitude and certain other ecclesiastical misgivings, it refused to join, preferring to work alone on its denominational work." David Craig, "L'E.R.Q. à cinq ans," 1 [translation mine].
    63. Sermons 793, 794, 797, E10.

CHAPTER TEN

Slowing Down and Moving Forward

CONTINUING FORWARD

Despite his difficulties with the decisions of The Presbyterian Church in Canada, David continued the work of pastor and evangelist in Trois-Rivières. Yet, and this quite apart from the forced separation from The Presbyterian Church, it was much more difficult to attract people to church in Trois-Rivières than it had been in Quebec City. He was not alone in noticing this slowdown. All over Quebec the booming time of revival for the evangelical churches had slowed down to a mere trickle. Some think that the revival slowed down because of the poor quality of leadership in the evangelical churches, but David too experienced this slowdown in his own ministry.[1] Much more important were the changes in Quebecois society as a whole during these years. The openness to new forms of spirituality in the mid-1970s had grown to cold scepticism.[2] People outside of the church were much

---

1. Some frustration about the work in Quebec is seen in the "Report to Classis Eastern Canada [of the Christian Reformed Church] from *Église Réformée du Québec*" (7 Mar. 1990). The report gives numbers from all the churches but often notes that evangelisation is 'difficult' and 'very slow.'
2. On this slow down see Richard Lougheed, "Le Réveil: L'arrêt du Réveil," in: *Histoire du Protestantisme au Québec depuis 1960: Une Analyse Anthro-*

less interested in what the church had to offer. The ministry committee of the E.R.Q. noticed this slow-down and the strain it could have on pastors, so initiatives were proposed to encourage pastors.[3] In both Trois-Rivières and Repentigny, David preached a sermon in which he stated that he thought the E.R.Q. needed a revival.[4] David thought that like any worthwhile structure, building a church takes time.[5]

Throughout this difficult period, David thankfully still enjoyed the support of his family. Ever since the beginning of their marriage Nancy had been a strong supporter of David's work as a pastor. She wrote letters, made phone calls, taught women's Bible studies and was always helping David welcome visitors into their home. Further, David loved being a father, and his relationship with his children was important to him. Church work put a great deal of pressure on him, but he always found time to be involved in his children's lives. He loved to play with them, laugh with them, and just be with them, whether it was eating an ice cream cone or enjoying a Big Mac with them. The presence and unconditional love that so characterized David's ministry were also

---

pologique, Culturelle et Historique, eds. Richard Lougheed, Wesley Peach and Glenn Smith (Quebec: La Clarière, 1999), 101–119.

3. *Comité du Ministère*–Rapport au Synode, "The committee is worried about the lack of contact between our congregations, about a certain lessening of enthusiasm for the mission of Jesus Christ among us and the tiredness that can set in among the pastors and elders in our congregations. It is our recommendation that the Synod designate one pastor from among us to visit our pastors and elders on a regular basis to encourage and solidify the links between our churches. The choice of the committee for this ministry is Jean-Guy deBlois, who can make himself available once a month to make such visits. It will also be necessary to give him a budget to cover the travelling and lodging expenses." D. Craig, J. Dufresne, J. Zoellner (26 Mar. 1994) [translation mine].

4. Sermon 693. For a similar opinion see sermon 701. See also sermon 284.

5. Sermon 457 and 718. See also Nancy's comments in letter to friends (Aug. 1988).

obvious in his relationship with Nancy and his children.[6] There were many and frequent challenges in his pastoral work, but he considered his wife and children to be his anchor.

Indeed, with such strong support and despite the difficulties these years brought, David continued making personal contacts in Trois-Rivières, giving Bible studies at church and teaching at Farel. In fact, he became "academic director" at Farel in 1992. In addition to continuing as professor of theology and church history, David also chaired the newly formed academic committee which was responsible for curriculum development and maintenance of academic standards. He was sent out to congregations to represent Farel and raise needed funds for the continuation of Farel's work.[7]

Furthermore, both David and Nancy became involved in the foundation and activities of the World Religions Museum in Nicolet (a small town just across the St. Lawrence River from Trois-Rivières). The project was conceived in the early 1980s and was meant to showcase the variety and traditions of religion in Quebec. Earlier exhibitions had met with some success,[8] and the museum was finally open to the public in its full form in August 1991.[9] Nancy helped in presenting the Protestant tradition and served as vice-president of the administrative council. She was very positive about the work of the Museum: "It represents an excellent means of education which will allow the public to know more about Protestantism. In coming to the museum, one can also learn that the Protestant Church is part of the universal 'Catholic' church

---

6. For the perspectives of his children on his life see: "A la mémoire de David Trevor Craig, 1937-2001," *En Lui*, special number (Mar. 2002): 3–5.

7. "New Academic Director," *Communiqué* (Fall 1992): 2.

8. See David's smiling face in a photo taken at one of these earlier exhibitions: Rita Dolan-Caron, "La prémière exposition du Musée des Religions de Nicolet: Témoignages d'appréciation des spécialistes," *Le Nouvelliste* (3 Nov. 1986): 5. In these earlier meetings David was refered to as a representative of the 'Presbyterian religion'.

9. "Musée des Religions: Centre international d'exposition," *Le Nouvelliste* (2 Aug. 1991): 1–20.

like the Roman Catholics."[10] David continued his involvement with the museum as a participant in a multi-religion discussion evening in 1993. This meeting was not to reduce the various religions (representatives of Judaism, Islam, Hinduism and Catholicism were also present) to those points on which they could agree, but simply "to get to know each other better". David was happy to note that as a Protestant he was not simply there to protest *against* something, but witness *for* the truth.[11]

During these years David implemented a program in the St-Matthieu Church called "La Serre."[12] This program consisted of small-group Bible studies, much like the "Koinonia" groups at St-Marc, aimed at building the spiritual maturity of his church members.[13] These groups were very important in creating durable links and common identity among the church's members. He knew that although the history of Protestant churches elsewhere was very long, their work in Quebec was very short. Hence, he was more conscious that good foundations (strong relations based on a common biblical theology) needed to be laid for durable results.[14]

Besides these special programs and activities, David was also involved on a daily basis in listening to, comforting, encouraging and exhorting the members of his congregation. Many appreciated David's ability to encourage them in the face of seemingly insurmountable obstacles. Others appreciated his ability to explain complex issues in simple language. Most noted that despite his poor organizational skills, he could keep people excited and programs moving forward.

---

10. *Le Nouvelliste* (2 Aug. 1991): 2.

11. Isabelle Légaré. "Au Musée des religions de Nicolet: la rencontre des croyances," *Le Nouvelliste* (31 mars 1993).

12. These studies were based on the English "Greenhouse" materials, a Reformed discipleship program developed by an elder and his wife at Coral Ridge Presbyterian Church in Fort Lauderdale, Florida. Nancy translated the material into French. See letter to friends (Jan. 1987).

13. See news of the St-Matthieu church in *La Vie Chrétienne* (Dec. 1986): 16.

14. Sermons 457 and 718.

In the present biography it is not possible to detail David's work in confidential pastoral matters. Yet, it was his acts of encouragement and his presence in these situations that most characterized his work as pastor wherever he went. Some have recounted publicly how David worked in their lives in these very intimate situations, but many others have kept these memories private.

In early 1994 David announced to his congregation in Trois-Rivières that he was taking the call to Repentigny. At the end of a sermon on Joshua 1, he addressed his congregation with regret and hope in his voice:

> Ten years ago Nancy and I came to St-Matthieu. We have lived highs and lows—by God's faithfulness throughout. We have learned to love each of you profoundly. You know that we have received a call from [the Reformed Church of] Repentigny. After much reflection and prayer we have decided to accept this call. Like Joshua we need to be reminded of God's faithfulness—and you as well. "I will never leave you—St-Matthieu Church—for you are mine [says the Lord]." Think of Joshua. Have the same attitudes that he had. May the Lord be our strength. Amen.[15]

Consequently, after almost a decade in Trois-Rivières he moved upstream to Repentigny in the suburbs of Montreal.

MOVING UP RIVER

At Repentigny he replaced Rev. Francis Foucachon who moved on to missionary work in France and elsewhere.[16] Reformed work in Repentigny began in 1984 when three couples from Montreal who wanted to make a difference in their milieu settled there. At first these couples and others like them joined in a small group assisted by visiting pastors. In 1987 they received the full-time help of Foucachon, an ordained missionary. On 15 November 1987 the first celebration of the community

---

15. Sermon 768.
16. The details of his call are discussed in (E.R.Q. PV 19940618): 5.

with their new pastor took place in the Foucachon's basement. The *Église Chrétienne Réformé de la Rive Nord* (known as the *Église Réformée St-Paul de Repentigny* after 1996) became an official member of the *Église Réformée du Québec* in 1988.

Years later, in the spring of 1994, David started serving the community all the while still living in Trois-Rivières. He traveled between the two communities on a regular basis staying with a family in Repentigny whenever necessary. He was officially installed as pastor on 19 September 1994.[17]

During this time David was on the lookout for a house that would be suitable for the needs of his family and the church. As in Trois-Rivières, David and Nancy were blessed with a 'miracle' of a house in Repentigny. In fact, the former occupant was bankrupt and forced to leave. He was so angry in leaving that he completely tore out anything of value from the house. The house being gutted, the bank sold this large house to David and Nancy for a very low price.[18] Although it needed much renovation, they bought it knowing it would serve the church in Repentigny well. Indeed, they hosted many church functions and guests in this residence on the bank of the Assomption River. Further, the congre-

---

17. Johanne Paiement, "Il était une fois . . . (la suite):" *La Source* 11 (Jun. 2003): 2–3.

18. David recounts this story in sermon 681. Nancy writes in a letter to friends (Christmas 1995): "In December 1994, we sold the house (four little neutral words behind which hide the pain of leaving a house that had been a real home for eleven years) and in February 1995, God led us to an unbelievable house here in Repentigny: a repossessed house on the Assomption River. The previous owner had been so angry at the bank that he literally stripped the house of everything except the furnace! He took the kitchen cupboards and appliances, flooring, doors, baseboards, woodwork, lights, toilets, sinks, bathtub, fireplace, chimney, interlocking bricks: you name it, he took it and what he couldn't take, he broke!! But the location was good, it had potential, it was an investment, it presented a huge challenge and it was cheap! So, in spite of some friends who thought we were crazy, we bought it!"

gation also moved its Sunday services to the *Centre Académique de Lanaudière*—only a few steps from the Craigs' new front door.

From the beginning the church focused on regular Bible studies, an emphasis on relationship-building and a desire to make the Gospel known to others in their community. Françis encouraged the "Pause-Café" outreach meetings and the use of the "Evangelism Explosion" materials produced by the Florida-based Rev. D. James Kennedy.[19] The group was young and somewhat fragile (finances were sometimes tight), but it quickly became well-rooted in the community with a membership of strong (and growing!) families. When the Foucachons arrived in 1987 there were 10 adults and 10 children; by September 1990 there were 21 adults and 21 children.[20] David, then, inherited a congregation which had several young families with a great number of children. Inheriting a church with several young familes and a number of children was a unique challenge for David because this was the first place in Quebec in which he did not have to establish the various ministries.[21] The church was already well-planted under Rev. Foucachon, though David continued to encourage the members to do outreach in the community.[22]

As elsewhere, David's messages focused on God's gift of grace, being one in Christ and the power of the Holy Spirit to move his hearers forward in the Christian life. He also put a great deal of stress on coordinating the evangelistic efforts of the church. Many Bible studies he organized were focused on learning skills and becoming

---

19. Kennedy's church, the Coral Ridge Presbyterian Church, was part of the P.C.A., the same denomination that sent Francis out as a missionary.

20. See "L'Église chrétienne réformée de la Rive-Nord: historique, vision et développement du projet" [report submitted for discussion ca. Sept. 1990].

21. Sermon 141 is the introduction to a brain-storming session David had with the three founding families of the Repentigny church.

22. Sermon E71. Nancy notes in a letter to friends (Christmas 1995): "We never cease to be amazed at how varied and exciting our life has been. 'Living on the edge under the direction of God' seems to be David's motto! Our life is again in flux as we settle into a new ministry."

motivated to do local evangelism. In the early years he did studies on "Making Christ known together!"[23] and "Being Witnesses to the People of Repentigny."[24] For these studies he introduced the subject with an interesting anecdote and biblical truth, and then asked questions based on the Bible readings.

A major tool for church unity and growth was the promotion of the 'Life' groups or, les groupes 'V.I.E.'.[25] In 2000, David reiterated the importance of these small groups for the life of the church.[26] In this presentation he noted that these 'life' groups had been formed for two reasons: (1) the stress and loneliness of those in our society and (2) the call of the gospel to have an up-building and unified community. "Biblically speaking," David remarked, "a healthy church is a community where the members love each other, where they help each other, where they pray together, socialize together, learn together, which is a family. This is the biblical image."[27] David noted that these groups were not simply a ministry of the church to others, but were a continuation of sorts of the Sunday morning celebration.[28] These groups not only gave the church community the opportunity to speak openly about the gospel, but also to serve each other in action.[29]

During his time as pastor the church started to give the Alpha course and the "Just Me and the Kids" program, a support group based on gospel principles for single-parent families.[30] Both of these were clearly

---

23. Bible study series: "Faire connaître le Christ ensemble!" 1997–1998. See sermons 10 and 372 for more of an introduction to this particular year's theme.

24. Bible study series: "Témoins envers le monde de Repentigny."

25. David explained that V.I.E. meant not only 'life', but 'Vérité', 'Intercession' and 'Evangélisation'—'Truth,' 'Intercession' and 'Evangelisation'.

26. Sermon 144.

27. Sermon 144 [translation mine].

28. See also sermon 613.

29. See sermon 449.

30. See Line Bilodeau, "Singulière aventure que celle de Pour Moi et mes enfants," *La Source* 11 (Jun. 2003): 5–7 and the continuation of this article in

meant to bring others in from the outside. Further, the "Just Me and the Kids" program was an effective way to show the community that the church was ready to serve and not to be served.[31] David constantly highlighted that God's grace motivated his children to be inclusive and loving and not divisive or schismatic. As such, he often preached on mutual encouragement and unity.[32]

David also gained great encouragement from participating in overseas missions projects in the final years of his life. In 1999 he went to Senegal to teach Reformed theology at the invitation of Jeff Marlowe.[33] He also went twice to Myanmar to participate in the young Reformed work there. He was not able to bring much with him in the way of resources, but he found great opportunities to serve the Lord.[34] These trips also further convinced him of the radical difference between the 'world' and the kingdom of God. This rejuvenated his desire to seek out and teach those who had never heard the good news.[35] He was planning to take another trip to Myanmar in January 2002.[36]

La Source (Dec. 2003): 6–7; See also Philippe Beauchemin, "Aide aux familles monoparentales: l'Église réformée offre des services," *Journal l'Artisan* (24 Jan. 2001): 13.

31. Sermons 11, 641.

32. For example, sermons 188, 207.

33. Sermon 428. See also Johanne Paiement, "Notre Histoire . . . la suite jusqu'à aujourd'hui," *La Source* (Dec. 2003): 3–4. Further, see Nancy and David's letter to friends (Jan. 2000).

34. See sermons 552, 629 and 639.

35. Sermon 632 and 636.

36. See letter to friends (22 Oct. 2001).

CHAPTER ELEVEN

At Rest

Just a few days before David's passing, Nancy wrote a newsletter to her family and friends. She thanked the Lord for her relationship with David:

> Even as we miss our children [they had both moved out by this time], we are delighted to be 'just two' again. We enjoy each other's company enormously. David has a wonderful sense of humour and keeps me laughing constantly. We have time to 'be in love'! We work hard, don't take many holidays but we are having fun being together and doing stuff together and after all, isn't that the way it should be?! Again, we are thankful to the Lord for preserving our couple.[1]

Alas, it was in Repentigny on 24 October 2001 that David passed away quite unexpectedly.

For some years David had been under the care of doctors for heart-related problems. He had always tried be physically active throughout his life, but he was genetically predisposed to heart troubles. Those around David started to see signs of extraordinary strain in the weeks and days prior to his death. A colleague at Institut Farel noted that David was 'pale as a ghost' and totally breathless after climbing the several flights of stairs in the newly renovated Farel building in downtown Montreal

---

1. Letter to friends (22 Oct. 2001).

in early October.² Further, Nancy noticed that he was totally breathless after a short trip up the stairs with some suitcases just days before he died.

Wednesday the 24th of October began as most others. That morning he had a pastoral visit with two congregation members. He and Nancy said goodbye to them on the driveway, and as they drove away Nancy volunteered to make tea as David walked behind the house to do some chores. After a few minutes Nancy entered the indoor swimming pool area in the back of the house and saw that David was lying on the ground. At first she thought this was a practical joke (he loved to play jokes on her), but when she called his name he was unresponsive. Nancy tried to resuscitate him, but he could not be brought back—all arteries to his heart were blocked. The man with whom she had shared so many joyful and challenging adventures was gone.

At his funeral, which was held in the facilities of the Erskine and American United Church in downtown Montreal with several hundred people in attendance, many emotionally expressed their appreciation for this modern missionary. As a member of the Canadian armed forces, the flag of Canada was draped over his coffin. Further, the lieutenant governor of Quebec, the Honourable Lise Thibault, made a special effort to attend the funeral. She was not too familiar with French Protestantism, but she had a special fondness for David and his work as her aide-de-camp.³ Her presence among so many friends and family members made the event very memorable.

Several months after the funeral, a special issue of *En Lui* magazine was published containing the speeches by the participants.⁴ Many pointed out that David Craig was a man with great energy and vision.

---

2. The student residence at Farel would be renamed the "Résidence David T. Craig" at its official opening in November 2001.

3. In fact, her presence at David's funeral delayed her arrival at another pre-arranged gathering by about two hours.

4. "A la mémoire de David Trevor Craig, 1937–2001," *En Lui*, special number (Mar. 2002): 25 pp.

AT REST

Others noted that he was a model missionary and community-builder. All emphasized his love and respect for people.

One man, who was influenced by David in Quebec City, said that David was an enthusiastic supporter of new French evangelism.[5] Another, who was a parishioner of David's in Trois-Rivières, noted that he was always ready to abandon his schedule to serve someone in need.[6] A third, a parishioner in Repentigny, revealed that David was for him a friend, a confidant and a spiritual father. Finally, even though her heart was broken, Nancy remembered that David was a missionary, a pioneer, a founder, a man of vision, a professor, a friend, a Christian brother, a caring pastor and a committed father and husband, all thanks to the faithfulness and grace of God.

David was buried in the cemetery at the Cuthbert Chapel in Berthierville, Quebec, on 29 October. Built in 1786, Cuthbert was the oldest Protestant chapel in the province.[7] As one who loved Protestant history, David was convinced he wanted to be buried in its cemetery. This, however, was not the first time David had been to Cuthbert. In 1998 he led a special service in the chapel where he preached a rousing message on humanity's death in sin and God's grace bringing one alive.[8]

At the burial several others spoke of David's dedication and kindness. A member of the Trois-Rivières church asked Nancy for a special request—he wanted to drape the flag of Quebec over David's casket. This gesture was to symbolize that David should be remembered as a man who dedicated a quarter-century of his life to working among

---

5. "A la mémoire de David Trevor Craig," 6.
6. "A la mémoire de David Trevor Craig," 8.
7. See the brochure: "La Chapelle des Cuthbert" (La corporation du Patrimoine de Berthierville Inc.). James Cuthbert was a high-ranking officer for General Wolfe (the general who invaded Quebec in 1759). He built the chapel in Berthierville to honour his wife at her death. The chapel became public property in the 20th century and can be visited by tourists.
8. Sermon 190.

the French-speakers of Quebec. Nancy wholeheartedly agreed to this request. Hence, David was buried under the fleur-de-lys.

ABOVE: David as a boy, ca. 1945

RIGHT: David at Waterloo Lutheran University, ca. 1961 (Used with permission of Paul Reader)

BELOW: Marriage of David and Nancy, 18 December 1965

```
TELEGRAM                    Canadian Pacific
                            429 0110        OCT 25 1967

ZC CPA781 ZC VIA CANADIAN
TBM360 TLWA47 MC1864                    1967 OCT 24 PM 9 23
CATO HG NGLS 014
LAGOS 14 24 2220
        PRESBYTERIAN CHURCH IN CDA
GLT  1342 50 WYNFORD DR DON MILLS ONT

PRESBYTER TORONTO
GREETINGS FROM LAGOS NARROW ESCAPE SAFE LETTER
FOLLOWS AWAITING INSTRUCTIONS
    DAVID
                        RECEIVED AT 1656 VICTORIA PARK AVE.
                              SUITE 1
                        TELEPHONE PL. 9-4471
```

ABOVE: David preaching at a wedding in Neuchâtel, Switzerland ca. 1972

LEFT: David posing for *Weekend Magazine* reporter in his traditional Nigerian wrap-around, ca. Jan. 1968. (Used with permission)

OPPOSITE PAGE:

(ABOVE) Telegram sent to Presbyterian Church in Canada offices by David in October 1967. (Used with permission of the PCC Archives)

(BELOW): David in the Alps, ca. 1970

ABOVE: Église St-Marc and manse in Ste-Foy, Quebec, ca. 1980

BELOW: Closing benediction of E.R.Q. pastors at the denomination's inauguration, 6 November 1988 (David is fourth from the right)

ABOVE: Padre Craig on training exercise with the Canadian Armed Forces

BELOW: David with his bees

ABOVE: David in pulpit of Cuthbert Chapel, ca. 1998
BELOW: David and Nancy, ca. 2001

PART II

The Thought of David Craig

CHAPTER TWELVE

A Missionary's Theology

INTRODUCTION

Wise counsel will tell us that "ideas have legs"[1], meaning they have a phenomenal power to shape our world, often in ways we take for granted. Once a person starts to wrestle with ideas, he or she can be profoundly transformed. Such was the case with David Craig.[2] David knew that ideas were not simply the stuff of an 'ivory tower', but were put into practice consciously or unconsciously. Often extremely powerful destructive ideas are accepted by society without it even noticing them.

David was not a seminal philosopher or theologian. In fact, I have not yet met any card-carrying 'Davidians' or 'Craigists'. He was, however, a man who held and wrestled with deep theological insights. His main concern was to model a positive, biblical Christian faith for 'ordinary' people like himself. Sometimes this meant breaking down the unhelpful and dangerous identity of the person he was trying to reach; most often, however, it meant picking up the pieces of a poorly-

---

1. Albert Wolters, *Ideas have legs* (Toronto: Institute for Christian Studies, 1987).
2. See sermon 617.

formed or broken identity. Throughout his life David consistently shared what he considered a biblical identity founded on God's grace and centred on Jesus Christ.

Interestingly, David left little in the way of printed resources to characterise his thought. Some of what was published is reproduced in this volume. These published articles represent only a fraction of what he presented orally in his life. Several other sources are a rich mine of his thought and personality. David kept most of his preached sermons, bible studies and course lecture notes. His preached sermons are almost all in complete paragraphs—both in English and French. His course lecture notes and Bible studies were usually written in point form. Most often the points are in almost complete phrases, but often enough he simply wrote a word or phrase—mostly little anecdotes, jokes or asides. The meaning of these little words and phrases are usually clear, but occasionally someone might need to ask around for an accurate interpretation. For example, I was quite puzzled by the phrase "non-practicing vegetarian" in several of his sermons.[3] He would simply write this without explanation. In my conversations with some of his former parishioners, I was informed that this was David's response to those who would tell him that they were "non-practicing Christians." David would say with a smile on his face that he was a "non-practicing vegetarian" to show them the false logic of a "Christian" who does nothing.[4]

It is potentially misleading to categorize the thought of anyone based on scattered notes or lectures. One can presume that he said much more about many subjects than what can be found in written form. Yet, with the number of sermons and lectures available, one can get a really good idea. David, like any preacher, had subjects that he felt were particularly important—we know this because he repeated himself a lot.[5] He believed that certain ideas, examples and biblical texts needed

---

3. E.g. sermon E95.
4. David seems to have borrowed this image from Francis Foucachon.
5. Sermon 507. David mentions here that even Jesus had themes in his

to be explained on different occasions or in different words on many occasions. Repetition, then, did not diminish the vitality of his message, it focused it.

THE WORD OF GOD AND THE IDEAS OF MEN

In order to create a biblical identity, David knew it was important to recognize the authority of Scripture. This authority came from his conclusion that the Word of God made flesh was directly related to the written Word of God. Otherwise stated, there is a distinction to be made between the two, but not a separation. Jesus Christ is the Son of God revealed from the Father, and the written Word is the will of God revealed from the Father. Both are from the Father and totally reliable. In accord with the Westminster Confession, David stated that Scripture's authority is based on its own internal testimony and the work of the Holy Spirit.[6]

Consequently, we do not wonder why David was so uncomfortable with the neo-Orthodox theologians whom he perceived as separating Jesus Christ from the written Word. In David's understanding the written Word is not simply a 'witness' to the Word, but it is the Word itself.[7] The import of this understanding is that the written Word ought not be added to, taken away from or contradicted in its teaching. David was concerned that modern thinkers (both liberal and more charismatic) not add to the Word of God based on modern ideas or extrabiblical revelation.[8] He believed that when anything is added to Scripture's

---

preaching that would come back with regularity.

6. Sermon 211.

7. Sermons 170, 500. He spends a great deal of time establishing this fact in his notes in his "Introduction au Nouveau Testament" course taught in the early years of his ministry at St-Marc's Church in Quebec. David says that Barth makes a false distinction between the living Word and the written Word. The Bible is not, says David, simply a witness to the truth, but is the truth itself.

8. Sermon 309, 724.

message, that message is always modelled on the theologian's image rather than on the image of Scripture.[9]

David was criticised for this position as one of 'bibliolatry'. Such critique sounds 'pious' because it seems to guard the place of Jesus Christ. But when examined more closely, thought David, this 'pious' critique is actually very destructive and false.[10] David underlined that this understanding of the close relation between Scripture and Christ comes from Jesus himself! David's understanding was that the church ought to have the same respect for the inspiration and authority of Scripture as did Jesus.[11]

For David, Scripture was both inspired and authoritative. It was inspired because it was breathed by the Spirit of God and written by the hands of prophets and apostles.[12] The Spirit did not use these men as simple automatons, but used their unique situations and abilities to compose the various texts of the Bible. By the Spirit, God's Word was accommodated to human understanding. The Bible is divine truth, but it is on a level which human beings can comprehend.[13] Nevertheless, Scripture is one whole and has one message.[14]

Because the Bible is the actual Word of God, it has an ultimate authority in life.[15] Recognizing the Bible's authority will help us read it the correct way. The same Spirit that inspires the Bible makes it known to the hearer.[16] We ought not approach it with a hard heart and a stubborn attitude, but with the intention of following it.[17] The Word of God ought to be our soul's nourishment. Further, true wisdom is

---

9. Sermon 407.
10. Sermon 579.
11. Sermon 579.
12. Sermons 99, 271.
13. Sermon 734.
14. Sermon 648.
15. Sermons 7, E44.
16. Sermons 51, 739.
17. Sermons 7, 268, 494, 511, 620, 630.

A MISSIONARY'S THEOLOGY

the ability to apply God's Word to one's life.[18] Scripture is the only true 'sword' by which we can fight the fierce spiritual battles in which we are engaged.[19] Scripture is a precious thing for which we must stand up and put our lives on the line.[20]

David did nuance his thought on why one should believe Scripture. It is not simply because God says it is true, but because it is historical *fact*.[21] For example, David explained that the fulfillment of the promises of the Old Testament in the New Testament attest to this factuality. In this context he notes, "hence, even in their smallest detail, the Bible is historically exact."[22] This respect for the historicity of the biblical text captured David's attention at many points in his life. He would on occasion distribute to his parishioners and students news clippings of recent scientific discoveries which confirmed the narratives of Scripture. His point was not necessarily that one *needed* science to confirm Scripture, but that Scripture was not *necessarily* anti-scientific.

Most clear among the facts of Scripture are the life, death, resurrection and ascension of Jesus Christ—fully divine and fully human. His presence is the fact *par excellence* of Scripture. For this reason, said David, when modern preachers and theologians start to question the reality of Christ's divinity, their teaching crumbles. On numerous occasions David warned his parishioners and students to beware of the dangerous teaching of modern liberal theologians.[23] On Easter 1988, David exhorted his congregation in Trois-Rivières with these words:

---

18. Sermon 47.
19. Sermon 176.
20. Sermon 287.
21. Sermons 64, 80, 139, 238, 422, 602, 711. See also the lecture notes from his course "Survol de l'Ancien Testament." In these notes he criticises the teachers of 'higher criticism' who question the historical reliability of biblical narratives.
22. Sermon 422: "Alors, dans les plus petits détails –même, la Bible est exacte historiquement."
23. Clear references are in sermons 8, 53, 55, 59, 63, 80, 81, 118, 162, 192,

> How can I be sure [of Christ's death and resurrection]? God does not ask us to believe 'despite the facts'. To believe without basis is neither Christian, nor biblical. Biblical faith is not to 'leap into the void'! God always gives us sufficient foundation—always enough facts to ground our faith. So, what are these facts? The central fact above all others is the resurrection. If Jesus is truly resurrected, then his Word and all his actions are confirmed.[24]

Hence, the truths of Christianity are neither simply things from which a believer can pick and choose, nor the speculation of learned philosophers. Again, David remarks: "the resurrection is practical because it is objective. It is dealing with facts—not dreams or philosophies."[25]

Yet, David warned against those who downplayed not only Christ's divine power, but also his humanity. For instance, at every Christmas the church in Trois-Rivières would gather together a choir under the able leadership of Nancy to sing at the church and for various community organizations. One year, the choir sang the classic French Christmas

---

199, 215, 278, 236, 278, 280, 282, 288, 315, 332, 333, 339, 393, 294, 406, 407, 424, 425, 474, 500, 566, 598A, 598B, 612, 623, 635, 640, 643, 663, 664, 670, 704, 709, 718, 725, 776, E7, E62, E78. Further, among his notes are a stack of photocopies of an article written by the *Gazette* columnist Harvey Shepherd very positively reviewing the recent book of John Shelby Spong, *Born of a Woman: a Bishop Rethinks the Birth of Jesus* (San Francisco: HarperCollins, 1992). Spong questioned much in the original narrative of Christ's birth, especially Mary's virginity. David, no doubt, wanted to pass this article out to friends to show them what kinds of ridiculous things liberal theologians were saying. Harvey Shepherd, "Biblical revision from a bishop's chair: Spong offers a new take on the virgin birth, Christ's resurrection," *The Gazette* [Sept. 1993?].

24. Sermon 64: "Comment puis-je être sur? Dieu ne nous demande jamais de croire 'malgré les faits'. Croire sans base n'est ni chrétien, ni biblique. La foi biblique n'est pas 'un saute dans le vide'! Dieu nous donne toujours des fondements suffisants—toujours assez de faits pour fonder notre foi. Alors quels sont ces faits? Le fait central par excellence est la résurrection. Si Jésus est vraiment ressuscité, alors toute sa parole et toutes ces actions sont confirmés."

25. Sermon 63: "Donc, la résurrection est pratique parce qu'elle est objective. Elle traite des faits—non pas des rêves ou des philosophies."

A MISSIONARY'S THEOLOGY

carol "Un flambeau, Jeannette, Isabelle." In the second stanza, one line reads "Approchez! Que Jésus est charmant! Comme Il est blanc, comme Il est rose!"[26] David found these last words bizarre for it made Jesus into a Western European. So, when he got around to singing this verse, he would sing 'olive' instead of 'pink'. To him this better represented Christ's real middle-eastern roots. A fact of Scripture, thought David, was Jesus' being born of middle-eastern parents—to change this would be to deny Jesus' true humanity.

The whole of Scripture points to these central facts of salvation. David was a preacher who tried to tie Scripture's story together. His was a hermeneutic of promise and fulfillment, otherwise known as covenant theology. Scripture spoke in terms of covenant relationships which always began with the initiative of God and worked out for the salvation of humanity.[27] When he spoke most clearly he would speak of a covenant of works and grace, but also a covenant of redemption from eternity.[28] God promises victory and brings that victory about.[29]

The drama of this story often clearly shone through when David explained Scripture. In Old Testament texts he loved to confront his audience with the raw emotion of the participants in the text. He wanted his hearers to enter into the story of Scripture as if it were their own story—as if it was happening in front of them.[30] Very often he did

---

26. "Come near! Jesus is so charming! He is so white, he is so pink!"

27. Sermons 171, 261, 317.

28. David taught a popular course on covenant theology outlining the progress of this idea through Scripture. He argued that the "covenant concept is fundamental in Scripture and, hence, fundamental for the history and theology of the church. It was poorly understood in the Middle Ages, but revived in the period of the Reformation." David explains the covenant of works and the covenant of grace, pointing to the initiative of God in both. He also makes clear that there was a covenant of redemption in eternity by which there was a voluntary pact between the three persons of the Trinity. See also sermons 448 and 488.

29. Sermons 160, 161, 177.

30. For example, David elicits the emotion in the story of Joseph very well

sermon series intended to carefully examine specific chapters, books or topics in Scripture. If necessary, he would highlight a specific Hebrew or Greek word that gave further clarity and vitality to the message of the text.[31]

FREEDOM IN CHRIST

Highlighting Scripture's authority and Christ's divinity had great practical importance for David—nothing less than human salvation was at stake. Hence, he was not shy in calling his hearers continually back to the biblical foundation and ideal. Without a robust doctrine of the Word, David knew that it was difficult (impossible!) to say anything of any consequence about the human state and eternal hope.

David's message was not one of simple doctrinal orthodoxy, but *joyful* orthodoxy. In fact, he criticised some of his fellow Reformed believers who thought that the solemnity of the Gospel message meant the Christian must be constantly in a state of dourness or sorrow. David would heartily agree that the message was of grave consequence, but it was a message which rejoiced the heart and allowed the Christian to live with joy.[32] "The Bible," said David, "is a book of joy."[33] This joy was not a 'godly' sorrow (which certain Reformed thinkers would paradoxically argue), but it was also not a simple happiness: "'happiness' depends on our circumstances, but joy depends on something altogether different—it depends on a relationship with God no matter what the circumstances!"[34]

So much was joy important that David cited it as the most important mark of the church. That which distinguished a Christian from a non-Christian more than anything else was joy. True, a pure heart, doctrinal orthodoxy, an evangelistic spirit, a quest for unity in the

---

in sermon 68.
    31. For example, see sermon 62.
    32. Sermon 701. See also sermons 83, 281, 290, 304, 486, 684, 717.
    33. Sermon 78: "La Bible est un livre de joie."
    34. Sermon 645.

A MISSIONARY'S THEOLOGY

church and an attitude of love were other distinguishing characteristics of a Christian, but above all these was joy![35] Life will be filled with tears, but will always end in joy.[36]

A Christian could have such joy because in Christ he or she is free. One of David's favourite sermon illustrations was the Swahili cry of freedom: "Uhuru!"[37] He thought this cry was much like the Christian's response of praise to the good news of freedom in Jesus.[38] David's message was the one he found in Scripture and the confessions of the church.[39] Because of the original and continuing fall, human beings are slaves in sin. Such sin is not simply outward immorality, but a perversion of all human faculties. This perversion turns us away from God and merits the just judgment of God. Without help from another, we have no hope in this dark world.[40]

But David announced that there was another! The help came from Jesus Christ, who, although God, became like us to bear the burden of sin and liberate us from the eternal consequences of sin.[41] This was the reason Christ needed to be fully divine and fully human. David said, "Jesus knew our fundamental problem very well. He knew that we did not have the power to do anything to change our situation of slavery.

---

35. Sermons 19–23, 706.
36. Sermons 279, 361.
37. Sermons 131, 247, 459, 570, 633, 706, E40, E86. Sermon 706: "After many years of ministry, I believe that the worship of the people of God is the most important element of our lives" [translation mine].
38. Sermons 152A, 152B, 152C, 209.
39. Sermons 72, 706, 740.
40. Sermons 32, 589, 646.
41. This idea is in basically every sermon David preached. However, examples of more extended explanations of it are found in sermons 6, 76, 100, 127, 172, 190, 191, 426, 493, 527, 717, 764, E72.

This is why he went to the cross."[42] The cross and resurrection, then, claimed the ultimate victory over death and sin.[43]

By faith, Christ's gift is ours and we can stand before God in Christ with assurance.[44] True faith for David was not a simple knowledge that God exists, but also a confidence in him—a relationship with him.[45] We are declared righteous in Christ before God's judgment seat and can live with hope despite the fact that we are still pilgrims through this earthly life.[46] The freedom in Christ does not mean that we can live as we choose, but that we can live with clean hands and a pure heart according to the law of God—the law no longer simply shows us how far we are from God, but how we might live in gratitude before him.[47] True freedom is not a freedom to do what one pleases, but a freedom of conscience, obedience and knowledge—true freedom is to be a disciple of Christ.[48]

When free, the disciple of Christ has real arms with which to fight the very existent spiritual battles that are still to be fought in the Christian life. The Devil, sin and death continue to attack the Christian despite the reality of the war being won.[49] The Christian faith is not defeatist, but points out that the only arm is the sword of the Spirit—God's Word.[50] A battle must be fought, but not by one's own power.[51]

---

42. Sermon 233: "Jésus connaissait de près notre problème fondamental. Il savait que la force nous manquait de faire quoi que ce soit pour changer notre condition d'esclavage. C'est pourquoi il est allé à la croix."
43. Sermons 404, 574, 610.
44. Sermons 6, 27, 85, 90, 108, 134, 363.
45. Sermons 356, 441, 592, 688.
46. Sermons 528, 529.
47. Sermons E26, E34.
48. Sermon 570. See also sermons 388, 434, 503, 583, 593, 744.
49. Sermons 320, 322, 354, 361, 362, 400, 490, 608, 610, 683, 791. David notes in sermon 410 that he preached on this spiritual war in Eph. 6 for his very first public sermon.
50. Sermons 170, 254, 433.
51. Sermon 107.

It is this sword which allows the Christian to fight the good fight, but always by the power of the Spirit.[52] David made sure to highlight the Spirit's role in animating all spiritual life—without him the Christian can do nothing. To rely on the Spirit the Christian needs to communicate with God, through the Word and prayer.[53]

David frequently preached about the work of the Spirit—this particularly because many charismatic and Pentecostal churches in the French-speaking milieu had somehow claimed the Spirit for themselves. David was encouraged that such charismatics seemingly had a great deal of outward joy—but they often emphasized aspects of the Spirit's work which were not really biblical. Most troubling for David was the charismatic tendency to put the emphasis on the Spirit alone. David was convinced that in Scripture the Spirit always led one to worship Christ. The Spirit is indeed one of the persons of the Trinity, but his work is not simply to give mystical experiences. Rather, the Spirit brings the hearers to truly know the Lord of life. The Spirit brings freedom—freedom in Christ.[54]

"POST TENEBRAS LUX": FAREL AND THE FORK

To help explain the central message of freedom in Christ, David surrounded himself with good books. Already in seminary he loved to read, but his abilities were honed and focused during his studies in Reformation theology in Switzerland. It is little wonder that he was attracted to the life and thought of the French reformer and evangelist Guillaume Farel. Farel was raised in good Catholic fashion at the beginning of the 16th century. He went to study in Paris where he met Lefèvre d'Étaples who encouraged him to read Scripture.[55] Slowly

---

52. Sermons 439, 634.
53. Sermons 37, 226.
54. Sermon 170.
55. Sermons 289 and 308. In certain letters and documents, one notes that David was pleased that professor Philip Edgcumbe Hughes (who had limited involvement in the work in Quebec, including an article in *Parole*

he began to understand that the message he saw in Scripture was not the message he was hearing from Roman Catholic thinkers. He found great depth in the teaching of Martin Luther and began to preach the importance of justification by faith. He moved to various places, but finally had lasting impact in what is now French-speaking Switzerland, especially with the coming of Jean Calvin. From this protected area of Switzerland these Reformed thinkers could in turn have a great impact on France and, indeed, the world.

What David loved, especially, was Farel's attachment to preaching Scripture no matter what the cost. David saw a man who let his principles drive his actions—he did what he believed. Farel, then, was not a model in all things, but in that he consistently brought attention to Christ and was dedicated to evangelising *in French*. David could not help but admire Farel's sort of 'bulldozer' personality.[56] David often mentioned the Reformation motto inscribed in the Reformation monument in Geneva as a wonderful call of victory that ought to be remembered: "Post tenebras lux"–"after darkness, light."[57]

In most every teaching opportunity he would mention this key thought—that we are saved by God's grace alone. At his home church, in the classroom and on the road this central message was clearly taught. Often he would recount the story of Martin Luther's internal struggle—how Luther tried to gain his salvation by works only to be

---

magazine) had published a popular book on Lefèvre called *Lefevre: pioneer of ecclesiastical renewal in France* (Grand Rapids: Eerdmans, 1984).

56. Among his papers is a 20-page hand-written manuscript on Farel. Written on size A4 paper (not the standard 8 ½ x 11 inches common to North America), this was probably written while he was still in Switzerland and could have been the beginning of a dissertation. David had planned on writing about the ecclesiology of Farel so these pages could have been a rough draft of an introductory chapter.

57. Sermons 565, 614, 674, 726, E7. See also his notes from the course "Survol de la dogmatique biblique" taught at Farel. Here he argues that 'post tenebras lux!' reflects a central biblical claim that a human "can only believe after he has been enlightened by the Holy Spirit."

continually thwarted in his attempts to please God; how he finally found God's assurance by believing in Christ as his justice; and how he overturned the works-dominated church of his time by this biblical message. Certainly, outside of biblical revelation, this period of church history (including the confessions of the 16th and 17th centuries) was most influential on David's thought.[58]

Yet, his study of the Reformation also helped him better understand the problems in contemporary Christianity. The Reformation for David was basically a clash about authority—specifically between the authority of the Bible and that of Tradition. For David, Luther's initial break caused the church to fork into three prongs.[59] The first prong, represented by the Roman Catholic Church, was that of an over-emphasis on Tradition. The third prong, represented by those in the 'Anabaptist' position was an over-emphasis on particular parts of Scripture without any regard for the whole or the *good* tradition in Christianity. The second or middle prong posited the ultimate authority in Scripture, yet upheld what was good in the churches' tradition. This middle prong shared the great Reformation doctrine of 'sola scriptura' with the third prong, but was careful not to become 'biblicist' in its understanding of Scripture. David saw that those of this third group who vigorously pretended their doctrine was an exact replica of New Testament Christianity had actually (albeit unbeknownst to them) adopted a whole new set of traditions. These unspoken traditions in Anabaptist circles (here David included all baptistic groups) could often be as harmful as the Roman Catholic capital "T" Tradition. For the Roman Catholics, problematic teaching came in through the front door, for the Anabaptists it came in through the back door—in the end both had a problem in the house.

Although the modern historian might find the historical reality of the Reformation and modern church hard to fit into a three-pronged fork,

---

58. For example, sermons 80, 147, 243, 249, 270, 289, 299, 405, 472, 527, 565, 574, 595, 597, 611, 722A, 722B, 726, 734, E5, E11, E70.

59. See sermons 133 and 686.

this simple diagram proved very effective in helping David's students understand an enormously complex period of Christian history.[60] An example of this fork in action should help: According to Roman Catholic Tradition, one is justified by faith *and* works. According to David this was clearly not what Scripture taught. Scripture taught that justification was by grace through faith *alone*. Consequently, on this doctrine the Roman Catholic Church is clearly over-emphasizing the teaching on works that had developed during the Middle Ages to the detriment of biblical teaching.[61] On the other hand, David would say that the over-emphasis by some in the Anabaptist tradition (again, he is speaking here of all baptistic groups, especially those affected by the theology of the Arminians in the early 17th century) put far too much emphasis on human choice in salvation by highlighting certain texts in Scripture to the detriment of the myriad of other texts which spoke of God's sovereignty and election.[62] God always took the initiative in salvation and faith was always a gift. Hence, on this doctrine the Anabaptist Arminians are clearly over-emphasizing one seemingly biblical doctrine to the detriment of the rest of the Bible's teaching. In the end, both the Catholics (works) and the Anabaptists (choice) *added* something a human had to do to be truly right before God.

A LIVING CHURCH

As was noted, David said in one of his later sermons that early in his career he fought very hard for biblical and doctrinal purity, but later in his career he put more focus on unity and joy in the Christian community. David was greatly concerned about biblically faithful doctrinal teaching, but he was constantly preoccupied with the unity, fellowship and advancement of the church. Whether he was teaching

---

60. Sermons 162, 239. See also the notes of his courses on "Ecclésiologie" and "Ordre et Discipline Ecclésiastique" given at Farel.
61. Sermon 527.
62. Sermons 49, 165, 172, 248, 267, 329, 430, 431, 510, 518, 581, 590, E66.

A MISSIONARY'S THEOLOGY

Old Testament, New Testament, church history, theology, pastoral care or apologetics, he would always return to the foundational themes of the church. Abraham's relationship with God tells us something about the church; Paul's relationship to his congregations tells us something about the church; Guillaume Farel's dynamic personality tells us something about the church. David did not have quick fix solutions for every problem in the church, but he clearly saw biblical principles, attitudes and postures which ought to be seen in the church.

This focus on the church led to two seemingly paradoxical ends in David's life—David was both very inflexible and very flexible in his church life. On the one end David often butted heads with others who had conflicting visions of the future and structure of the church. David would shrug off their critique and stick to his ground. The clearest (and most painful) example was his refusal to support women's ordination to the offices of elder and pastor in The Presbyterian Church in Canada. David was convinced by his reading of Scripture that being male was one among many qualifications one must have to hold the offices of elder and pastor.

Paradoxically, however, we see in this situation that David was also very flexible. Although he rejected women's ordination to eldership, he would work informally with just about anyone.[63] It was in David's character to accept all as friends until the opposite was proven. Some might say this was naive or that he had an overly-gullible spirit, but the fact remains that this characterized his work for the duration of his ministry in Quebec. David was always a gatherer—he had a gift of gathering a disparate group of people around him to work on a

---

63. In a letter to his 'Uncle Art' in 1979, David mentioned that perhaps it would be possible to someday form some sort of a 'coalition' between the Brethren and Presbyterians. Letter (22 Feb. 1979). Further, in his early days at St-Marc's Church in Quebec, David would participate in unity marches with many other Christian denominations—including Roman Catholics. See sermons 268, 348, E35.

common mission. Sometimes this led to a certain amount of confusion, but as long as David was present the task could be continued.

Perhaps David's rigid/flexible ecclesiology can be best described in relation to his stress on the work of the Holy Spirit. Many have said that Jean Calvin was the "theologian of the Holy Spirit", and David Craig was certainly a follower in this regard. Particularly David noted that the Spirit called people together and kept them together.[64] While in Quebec, David stated this fact from the pulpit:

> I am kind of sad for churches where everyone is of the same social class and where everybody looks like cookies from the same package! One of the things I love about our church is that we all come from very different backgrounds. Look around you. Look at the beauty of our differences. French folks say, 'long live differences'—so, we Christians should say it as well.[65]

Great harm was done to the church when one caused division or confusion—it was nothing less than working against the Spirit.[66] For this reason David reminded his hearers of Augustine's adage of "humility, humility, humility" in all things of the church.[67] For David humility bred unity.

For David, this unity is best exemplified in a local church's fellowship.[68] Christians are called together irrespective of age, language, background, education, family choices, etc. We cannot choose our 'team'—the Spirit draws us into each other's lives in the bond of

---

64. Sermons 75, 677.
65. Sermon 690B: "Je suis assez triste pour des paroisses où tout le monde vient de la même classe sociale ou là où tout le monde se ressemble comme les mêmes biscuits dans un paquet! Une des choses que j'aime de notre paroisse est que nous venons des arrière-plans très différents. Regarde autour de toi. Regarde la beauté de nos différences. Les Français disent 'vive la différence'—alors nous les chrétiens devrions dire aussi."
66. Sermons 454, 455, 456, 487, 502, 507, 708.
67. Sermons 26 and 595. See also sermon 428.
68. Sermon 690.

fellowship—*Koinonia*.[69] Any 'Christian' who proposes some sort of a two-tiered system of church life—the 'more' and the 'less' spiritual groups—should strenuously be avoided. David exhorted his congregation members in this way: "We cannot be proud if we take stock of the fact that all that we have, we have received from the Lord. Hence, it is impossible to become proud. The more we live with the gratitude welling up in our hearts, the more we will be humble with our brother."[70] No matter how long a person has been involved in the church, he or she is still equal with all the others as a sinner saved by God's grace.[71]

But, thought David, what joy to be surrounded by other children of God who by no merit of their own have been called into a glorious kingdom![72] Rather than hiding in one's own corner, Christians were called to bear one another's burdens and make their 'neighbour' a priority. David knew that the church was not simply theoretically a 'body', but composed of members who *actually* cared for and complimented each other.[73] There are many different gifts in the body, but these gifts are given for the sake of the body and not the individual members.[74]

Further, a unified, cohesive church cannot but tell friends and neighbours about Christ's work.[75] Evangelism, then, was not simply an 'option' for the church. Explaining the gospel and welcoming new

---

69. Sermons 6, 22, 94, 103, 170, 586, 731, 732.

70. Sermon 75: "Nous ne pouvons être orgueilleux si nous nous rendons compte que tout ce que nous avons, nous avons reçus tout vient du Seigneur donc impossible de s'enorgueillir. Plus on vit avec la reconnaissance surgissant dans notre coeur, plus on serait humble envers notre frère."

71. Sermons 46, 163.

72. Sermon 36.

73. Sermons 6, 7, 11, 14, 15, 23, 22, 24, 46, 112, 117, 188, 189, 202, 207, 275, 320, 334, 387, 408, 445, 495, 522, 586, 641, 731, 732.

74. Sermons 130, 149, 223, 224, 225, 226, 292, 337, 338, 341, 344, 427, 689. See also his series of articles on spiritual gifts in *Parole* magazine listed in the bibliography below.

75. Sermon 732.

members into the church was a top priority for every member.[76] David often reminded his congregation that the pastor's job was not simply to do the evangelism, but more importantly to *encourage* evangelism.[77] He looked to the early church as a model community which was corporately engaged in announcing the good news.

Finally, David noted again that the freedom to progress as the church was not a freedom to do what one pleased, but was a structured freedom. David underlined the fact that there is a structure and discipline in the church so that it can continue on a safe and joyful path.[78] This informed his understanding of the offices of elder and deacon, of worship, of church activities and of the sacraments.[79]

Particularly, this freedom in order affected his teaching on marriage. David taught that besides one's public engagement to God and the church, the most important public decision one can make in life is the commitment to love one's spouse. Such commitment was between one

---

76. Sermon 335.

77. David frequently mentioned the church's task of evangelism. For examples, see sermons 9, 10, 12, 25, 27, 73, 138, 168, 209, 258, 336, 342, 349, 350, 419, 432, 437, 468, 586, 605, 664, 689, 710, 732.

78. Sermons 89B, 102, 217A, 435, 752-758.

79. Sermon 29. See also his lecture notes on "Ordre et Discipline Ecclésiastique." In these lectures he makes the distinction between a conception of church order based simply on 'tradition' and one which is based on a 'legalistic' reading of Scripture. David argued for a position based on the foundational principles of Scripture, but which took into account the society in which the church lived. David had a preferred vision for church government in Quebec, but he was ready to accept that other forms of church government were acceptable and still generally upheld the principles of Scripture. He was particularly critical of those churches who claimed their church form was based 'exclusively' on Scripture (i.e. it was a reproduction of the New Testament church). These groups (especially the Brethren, in which he was raised) might practice certain activities in a seemingly 'more' biblical manner, but they have an equal number of traditions in practice that are directly informed by the society in which they live. (Notes from course "Ordre et Discipline Ecclésiastique," 2–8).

man and one woman for life. In Scripture David found the teaching of the willing submission of the wife to the husband's spiritual leadership, and the husband's self-giving love to the wife. He knew that while all marriage relationships would be tested, they would also weather the storms when based on the biblical model and united in faith.[80]

READY FOR MINISTRY IN QUEBEC

David was conscious that the message of Scripture might not be very popular in Quebec—or anywhere else for that matter. He clearly saw that Quebecois society was often not respectful of the Christian faith or the biblical model of life.[81] Yet, he knew that the public rejection by those who seemed strong did not reflect the reality of life. His experience was that most people were quick to attest to pain, weakness and struggles through life.[82] Hence, most people craved the kind of love found only in God and his church.[83] Having such a perspective, David continued to announce the good news and model the life of a freed disciple.

---

80. David's teaching on marriage and family was continuous and extensive. For example, see sermons 74, 89, 89B, 92, 97, 109, 126, 151, 153, 154, 155, 156, 157, 167, 183, 184, 185, 186, 187, 216, 217, 217B, 218, 219, 230, 255, 256, 257, 262, 263, 264, 265, 277, 458, 469, 475, 489, 492, 554, 644, 647, 676, 697, 749.

81. Sermons 39, 50, 87, 142, 195, 208, 741, 774.

82. Sermon 67.

83. Sermons 63, 93, 678, 722A, 722B, E35, E42, E72.

CHAPTER THIRTEEN

"A Dialogue about Dialogue"

DAVID T. CRAIG

Presbyterian College Life (1965): 10–11.

Dr. Martin Lloyd-Jones once said: "Putting all the ecclesiastical corpses into one graveyard will not bring about a resurrection."

Protestantism, in a growing number of quarters, is in a state of decay. Theologians and bishops confidently assure us that God is in some way identical with man, that our world is "a closed naturalistic system" and that the first and greatest commandment is to love one's neighbour (Matt. 22:36–39). Sentimentalism, secularism, humanitarianism and even forms of anti-trinitarianism have replaced the genuine Christianity of the New Testament. Views ranging from crass literalism to exotic liberalism are accorded a hearing and are dignified as 'schools'.

Despite the internal chaos, or perhaps because of it, the corpses are being gradually, and in turn, loaded onto the Ecumenical Hearse and slowly driven to the family plot, all in the bright-eyed hope of the resurrection of medieval order and the renewal of spiritual power.

One does not willingly draw such a dismal sketch. But it is always wise to be realistic. Protestantism has lost its way and refusal to face the unsavoury fact with not be a service to Christianity. But the picture is not wholly black. God still has His 'seven thousand' who have not bowed the knee to Baal. Through His faithful remnant, He preserves and sets forth His truth from generation to generation. It was this faithful remnant that formed the heart of belief in ancient Israel. It is this remnant that forms the core of genuine Christianity in the church today. What then does the genuine Christian believe? A catalogue of dogmas by itself would be meaningless and sterile. Any spoken statement of belief must bear the 'incontestable witness of the Holy Spirit' who writes these truths on the heart and makes them a vital reality in everyday life.

Vital Christianity believes in:

1. The absolute supremacy of Almighty God, as Creator, Redeemer and judge of the whole world.
2. The finite fallenness of sinful mankind and his powerlessness to procure for himself whole or part of his own salvation.
3. The eternal existence and deity of Christ, the Son of God; His incarnation by the Holy Spirit of the Virgin Mary, the absolute, final sufficiency of His sacrificial death on the Cross as the atonement and satisfaction for man's sin; His actual resurrection from the dead in a glorified body and His actual ascension into heaven in that same body.
4. The reality of the power of the Holy Spirit, the third Person of the Trinity; the necessity for the Holy Spirit's dynamic transformation of the innermost part of a man in the 'new birth'.
5. The Moral responsibility of the regenerate man to live by the power of the Holy Spirit in the law and will of God.
6. The enlivening certainty of the personal coming again of Christ at the end of this age to judge the living and the dead and to complete the redemption He procured for us at Calvary.
7. Finally, and most importantly, as the basis for these beliefs, vital Christianity receives the Holy Scripture as authoritative and sufficient in all matters of faith, life and worship, as the Word of God. In it genuine Christianity has received binding definition by Christ Himself in the teaching given both through His own lips

A DIALOGUE ABOUT DIALOGUE

and through His prophets and apostles under the inspiration of the Holy Spirit. (2 Pet. 1:16–21)

In light of this, how ought we to view the current spirit of ecumenism?

It should be obvious that denominational lines are now anachronistic. Whether speaking of Rome or of our own particular brands of Canadian Protestantism, the scandal of our own divisions is not, as we are so persistently told to believe, the mere existence of separate denominations. The real scandal which cuts across all denominations and which is within each of them, is the absence of the 'Whole Counsel of God' from our pulpits. The uncertain sound of the trumpet at the moment of battle is confusing the army. There is much evidence that many are becoming heartsick with the husks and shallow uncertainties which too many Protestants have substituted for the eternal basic truths of our Lord's Gospel. At the same time, Roman Catholics are reacting deeply against an arid formalism and denial of personal assurance and peace with God that typifies the papal system. The new movement of Roman Biblical studies, as it is exemplified in Father De Vaux of the Jerusalem School of Biblical Studies, may well condemn philosophizing unbelieving pseudo-Christian Protestant theologians for their cowardly compromising and departure from sound Biblical truth.

Christ's seven thousand are still among us. They are the true ecumenists. Evangelicals with a high view and reverence for Holy Scripture, be they among Protestants or Roman Catholics, must seek each other out, rejecting the ambiguities of our current 'fashionable' dialogue and standing together, suffering if necessary for the Word of God and the testimony of Jesus (Rev. 1:9).

These are not destined for the ecclesiastical graveyard for they have within them the 'power of the resurrection'.

CHAPTER FOURTEEN

"The Protestant Witness in Quebec"

DAVID CRAIG

In: *Le témoignage protestant au Québec: Hier, Aujourd'hui, et demain.* Montreal: Senate of Presbyterian College, 1981.

At the outset, I would like to congratulate the Senate of the Presbyterian College for having chosen a topic which affects all of us who work in a Quebecois milieu.[1]

I would also like to transmit greetings from the Theological Seminary of Quebec. We have particular interest in this subject. Yet, we are not totally at ease with the theme—it is the word Protestant, but it is not because we are ashamed of this title, even if Joe and Mary on the street think that the word Protestant means a person without faith, who plays golf on Sunday morning and who lives without an inner spiritual life or prayer.

---

1. The title of the colloquy was "Le temoigage protestant au Québec: Hier, Aujourd'hui, et demain!" As David notes, it was organized by and held at the Presbyterian College in the late 1970s. The other participants were Dr. Irenée Beaubien, S.J. (Centre Canadien d'Oecuménisme), Rev. Hervé Finès (United Church), Rev. Denis Fortin (Lutheran Church) and Rev. Charles Odier (United Church).

In fact, it was in 1529 at the Diet of Speyer that reformers were first called Protestants. From 1517 to 1529 they were known by another term—a term which continues to be honourable at least in Europe: Evangelicals. This term meant a witness concerned to base all parts of his life on the Word of God. For them there was no doubt concerning the Word of God. The written Word, the incarnate Word and the dynamic Word, that is the Holy Spirit, were one WHOLE, a UNITY—a tri-unity or trinity which could not be divided. This foundation, the BIBLE sustained every part of their lives.

It was this kind of certainty which allowed the Huguenots, forced to undergo continual persecution, trials and martyrdom, to leave a powerful witness in the pages of church history.

Such a faith was not founded on doubtful Scripture, nor on the sometimes contradictory pronouncements of theologians. This faith was founded on unshakeable certainties, on the written Word of God.

Even though Norman Moiler does not share their faith, the Huguenots would have surely agreed with him when he said: "To be a man! Here is the life-long battle! We lose part of ourselves . . . of our integrity with every compromise that we make with an authority in which we have no confidence." The Huguenots had confidence in their authority. Scripture was their foundation and the last court of appeal.

The first attempts of the French to colonize North America happened during this struggle. France, temporarily open to Reformed influence, became increasingly a theatre of political and religious conflict brought up by the fundamental questions of the Reformation.

What is the ultimate authority? Is it the tradition of men personified in the Papacy or is it in the indivisible Word of God? The word incarnate, the written Word and the dynamic Word, that is, the Holy Spirit.

There are not thirty-six answers to this question!

It is at this point that Gaspard de Coligny, a Reformed leader and admiral in the French Navy under Henry IV, had the idea to establish a colony outside of France which would be a place of refuge for French Reformed believers. French Huguenots attempted settling in Brazil,

THE PROTESTANT WITNESS IN QUEBEC

Florida and Carolina—especially because it was becoming more difficult to live in the increasingly Roman Catholic dominated France.

It was also at this time that Tadoussac, Port Royal and Quebec were established. The main goal was to establish commercial centres to organize the fur trade, yet they also represented the first serious attempts to settle in the name of the French King.

François-Xavier Garneau was the first Quebecois author to insist on the importance of the Reformed at the beginning of New France. Above all, he questioned the rationale for excluding them from the colony in 1627 at the formation of the Company of One Hundred Associates, an organization formed by the Roman Catholic hierarchy to eliminate Huguenot privilege in the leadership and economy of the colony.

Garneau opened a can of worms! What he wrote expressed to the public ideas which went against the image created by the hierarchy of a New France entirely Roman Catholic.

Several passages, almost full pages of editions of Garneau's book which appeared in Quebec needed to be rewritten. There were even full pages cut out by the ecclesiastical censors! The goal, obviously, was to cover up any mention that Huguenots were important among the first founders of New France.

But being a shrewd historian, Garneau was wise enough to publish not only in Montreal where his book had been 'fixed', but also in Paris. The French version was not changed, hence it is easy to put the two editions side-by-side to see how the Roman Catholic censors changed his work.

But, let us come back to the beginnings of New France. In October 1540, Françis I gave the order to Jacques Cartier to instruct the Natives, and I cite, "in love and fear of God and of the holy law and Christian doctrine." Note that there is no distinction here made between a Roman Catholic faith or a Reformed Catholic or Huguenot faith. In January 1541 the King of France appointed Roberval, a Huguenot, as the first lieutenant-general of Québec, giving him this same mandate. Hence, until 1588, a period of 48 years, Huguenots had carte blanche to instruct "in love and fear of God and of the holy law and Christian doctrine."

But in 1588, the Catholic hierarchy, troubled by events in Quebec, managed to change the mandate given to Huguenots. For the first time the Huguenots are reigned in. Now the Roman Catholic faith was to be spread in Quebec. The instructions became, "to inculcate, root, and follow in the fear of God, the apostolic and Roman Catholic religion." This added detail comes back to exclude the Huguentos in all the decisions regarding the colony thereafter.

The context is obviously the Reformation which is making headway in all of France. The exclusion is obviously by those who took Roman Catholicism as a synonym for Christianity. Yet, in France there is still a fair bit of tolerance. It was under King Henry IV in 1598, that the Edict of Nantes assured the Catholic Reformed minority of a legal existence beside the Roman Catholic majority. This climate of toleration permitted Reformed merchants to operate colonial establishments even though they were supposed to be promoting Roman Catholicism. Hence, a strange situation resulted. For many years it was up to many Huguenots to plant the Roman Catholic faith in Quebec.

To other lieutenant governors like Chauvin in 1599 and de Mons in 1604, it was clarified that it was the Roman Catholic faith that was to be promoted. But this precision did not stop the Reformed from operating their colonial businesses as they wished. Even Samuel de Champlain was surprised. About the expedition of Chauvin he would write: "The problem in this expedition was that a task was given to a man who was of another religion, to impair the Catholic, apostolic and Roman faith, which the heretics despise and consider an abomination."[2]

---

2. "Ce qui fut à blasmer en ceste entreprise, est d'avoir donné une commission à un homme de contraire religion, pour pulluler la foy Catholique, Apostolique, & Romaine, que les hérétiques ont tant en horreur, & abhomination." Samuel de Champlain, *Oeuvres*, ed. C.H. Laverière, 2nd ed., vol. 5 (Quebec: Laval, 1870), 700.

Further, P. Chauvin, for example, no longer felt bound by this religious clause of his commission. He only brought pastors to the colony. Later on and under pressure, De Mons admitted a few priests into the colony. Because of this situation Louis Hébert, a Roman Catholic, asked a 'Lutheran' pastor to baptise his nephew. There was no Roman Catholic priest!

In these years, a certain pluralism of religions (Catholic and Reformed, of course) developed in Quebec. The Roman Catholics complained that they had to attend Reformed worship services so that they could be well respected as leaders of the colony. According to several different authors of that time, any religious harmony became rare, especially with the coming of the Jesuits.

Of course, none of this is spoken about in our school history texts . . .

The Huguenots saw the members of the Company of Jesus, the Jesuits for what they really were: champions of the Counter Reformation, sworn enemies of Reformed Catholicism. Already in France Reformed traders tried to stop the Jesuits from embarking on the ships bound for the New World. They managed to get on, but were not allowed to get off once in the New World. They were finally allowed to come off the ship when the Recollets vouched for them and housed them. This cold reception indicates the religious opinion that the majority of the colonists shared. Further, it shows the reason for which the Jesuits played such an important role in the exclusion of the Huguenots in the ensuing years.

In a series of meetings, letters sent to the King and pamphlets, the Recollets and Jesuits worked together with other Roman Catholics in the colony to exclude all Huguenot presence. Their arguments were simple and direct: The Huguenots are clearly heretical, they try to evangelize their compatriots with pamphlets, they encourage the reading of Scripture and they have radically changed the celebration of the Mass. Even more, all the problems of the colony have at their root the presence of this other religion and the commercial interests of the Huguenot merchants. The Huguenots did not come to encourage colonization.

One ought to note that the Reformed leaders were increasingly obligated to promote immigration of Roman Catholics to New France. Hence, there was automatically less interest in attracting new settlers who would eventually eliminate the privileges of the Huguenots in the colony.

In 1621, the important Roman Catholics in Quebec came together to propose to the King: "that the King not allow all persons who profess the supposedly Reformed Religion (Religion prétendue Réformée) to live here or to permit any persons from any nation whatsoever of this supposedly Reformed Religion on the pain of whatever is considered reasonable."

Three years later in 1624, Guillaume de Caën, a well-known Huguenot, lost his position as General of the navy and was barred from entering the Saint-Laurent. His brother-in-law, a Roman Catholic, takes the post in his place. In the same year a public book-burning happens in the centre of Québec of Calvinist books which were distributed to the Roman Catholic population.

Finally, in 1627 with the establishment of a Roman Catholic company to direct the commerce of Québec, the official exclusion of the Reformed is put in place. The commercial monopoly of the Huguenot de Caën is revoked and Quebec becomes officially Roman Catholic. This situation changes temporarily in 1628 with the arrival of the Kirk brothers—Protestants called by like-minded believers to save the Huguenot structure.

Yet, four years later Quebec is returned to France again by the English and the Huguenot era is officially dead . . . until 1759 when Wolfe and the English take over the colony.

In 1728, Baron de Lahontan,[3] wrote words that should help us think again about the decision to exclude Protestants from New France:

---

3. Louis Armand Delom d'Arce (1666-1715), better known as Baron de

THE PROTESTANT WITNESS IN QUEBEC

I am surprised that instead of getting rid of the Protestants from France, who fled to our enemies and caused great damage to the Kingdom by the money they brought with them to these countries and the industry they established in these places, that we did not send them to Canada. I am convinced that if we could have given them guarantees of freedom of conscience, many would have had no problem in settling there. Several people have noted to me that the remedy was worse than the problem since they would not have missed the opportunity sooner or later to chase away the Catholic with the help of the English.[4]

I think that in Quebec, as in France, we still suffer today from a refusal to be considered a nation of the Reformation. A philosophy or a theology always creates a certain way to view the world and reality. More than one theologian in the history of the church has noted that the actions of a people is determined by what they profoundly believe.

Thankfully, we are in an ecumenical age. It is good that many of the old battles are now behind us. Yet, several absolutely fundamental questions remain. These questions are ones which come from my religious roots to be sure, but they are nonetheless important for us all. Do we believe that a man is made righteous before God by faith in Jesus Christ with nothing added? Do we believe that man, even one who is well-educated, cannot be his own authority because we are all sinners? Even in Christ the person, as Luther said, is still a justified sinner. If

---

Lahontan, was a French explorer and anthropologist who created an immensly popular travelogue of the New World.

4. "Je suis surpris qu'au lieu de faire sortir de France les Protestants, qui passant chez nos ennemis ont causé tant de dommage au Royaume par l'argent qu'ils ont apporté dans leurs Païs & les Manufactures qu'ils y ont établi on ne les ait pas envoiez en Canada. Je suis persuadé que si on leur avait donné de bonnes assurances pour la liberté de conscience, il y en a quantité qui n'auraient pas fait difficulté de s'y établir. Quelques personnes m'ont répondu à ce sujet que le remède eut été pire que le mal puisqu'ils n'auraient pas manqué tôt ou tard d'en chasser les catholiques par le secours des Anglais."

this is the case, should we not ask ourselves the question of who is in authority? Who is worthy?

Our missionary activity ought to be a constructive work. The mission that we see in the New Testament was not simply for the Apostles to go around destroying idols and stopping all other forms of worship. It was rather to preach the Gospel.

The first Christians looked at their mission as something very positive. Their world was full of idols and in the hands of many different sectarian groups. Yet, we never read in the Gospels that they forced converts to conform to a Jewish gospel or a Greek gospel or a legalist gospel. They preached a positive Gospel—that of salvation in Jesus Christ, the Son of God, who was crucified, who rose from the grave and who ascended into heaven.

This sole teaching was enough to forget about the old idols and leave the pagan temples to fall into disuse.

Paul said that the Gospel is the power of God, a power that changes people like the Huguenots. The Reformed Church has traditionally founded its government on evangelical principles. This Church also announced grace, the good news to all those who listed and wanted to receive it.

Here is the path to follow in the Quebec of our times, a positive Gospel full of the power of the Spirit of God and based fully on Scripture. There are many methods to accomplish this task.

CHAPTER FIFTEEN

"The Power of the Spirit"

DAVID CRAIG

Parole (1985)

About 16 years ago, Christian communities started to become aware of a movement which developed in many denominations, first in the United States and then in Europe. The most characteristic mark of this new movement was its insistence on an experience described as the 'baptism in the Holy Spirit'. Many of this movement's fundamental principles were similar to those of Pentecostal Churches. Among traditional Christian denominations, those in this movement were known as 'neo-Pentecostals', but adopted more and more the name 'charismatics'.

In the beginning, the new movement appeared as a spontaneous organism, but after more in-depth research, it was clear that traditional Pentecostalism had a large influence on the charismatic movement. Frederik Dale Brunner, theologian and missiologist, notes that Protestant Churches, as well as Roman Catholic Churches since the Second Vatican Council, have been vigorously critiqued by many of their own members because of their perceived institutionalism and their lack of spiritual life. Speaking to these spiritually undernourished Christians, the neo-Pentecostals argue that the power for individual and church-wide spiritual life ought to be found in the baptism of the Holy Spirit, so long neglected, but which now has been rediscovered and experienced, especially in the manifestation of spiritual gifts. Each 'charismatic' is convinced that the reason for the vibrancy and rapid growth of the movement throughout the world is based on the truth of Acts 1:8: the power of the Spirit of God at work.

David Duplessis of the ecumenical council of churches in Geneva says:

> We believe that the benediction of the baptism of the Holy Spirit is as valid today as it was two thousand years ago when the Spirit first came. There is no mystery or secret here. The reason for our growth is not due to the abilities or education of the missionary, nor to new missionary methods. Rather, we exhort all new converts to receive the Holy Spirit in all simplicity in order to become a witness for Jesus Christ.

Here is, then, the question. For a member of the charismatic movement, there are two steps to be a Christian. The first is conversion which is the baptism by the Spirit of God and the second conversion which is the baptism in the Spirit. The nuances in the terminology are very important. If conversion is necessary, baptism in the Spirit is superior to baptism by the Spirit (conversion). The charismatic believes that the Spirit has baptised all sincere believers (conversion), but that Christ has not yet baptised each believer in the Spirit (the experience of the day of Pentecost). This second experience is distinct from conversion and happens only subsequently. Speaking 'in tongues' is the tangible proof of this second conversion, and it should be seriously sought after. Even more, it is argued that "we have neither the fullness nor the permanence of the Holy Spirit without this second experience of spiritual baptism."

We ought to examine these claims using several passages from Scripture:

THE POWER OF THE SPIRIT

1 Corinthians 6:11

The Apostle Paul here insists that the believer, purified from his past, becomes the possession of God, "by the name of our Lord Jesus Christ and by the Spirit of our God." Paul does not introduce any division between the work of Christ and the work of the Spirit. On the contrary, the name of Christ is mentioned with that of the Spirit.

John 3:5–8

The Gospel of John speaks clearly of the unity of the work of God (Father, Son and Holy Spirit) in this passage. This text is without doubt the classic description of Christian initiation. Jesus declares, "No one can enter the Kingdom of God if he is not born of water and the Holy Spirit."

According to the Gospel of God, there are two births: the one natural and the other spiritual. Hence, there is not a natural birth, a semi-spiritual birth and, finally, a fully spiritual birth. One must be born again, not 'again and again'. Spiritually, a person is born again one time, just like she is physically. The import of John 3:5–6 is put on the Spirit and his work. To be born again means a fundamental reworking of the person to the foundation of her person. How the Spirit accomplishes this work is not explained, nor how the link is made between his invisible and interior action and the visible sign of that action. Its context (John 3:8) ought to show us that we need not look for an overly-rigid link. We ought simply to know that the Spirit comes from above. How, when, where and why he does his work remain above our ability to comprehend.

Titus 3:4–8

In the letter of Paul to Titus, we have a résumé of the biblical teaching on the theme of the 'baptism of the Spirit'. The Apostle sees the whole event of salvation, from beginning to end, as one great action. Salvation is real because "God our Saviour manifested his goodness and his love for humanity." This work, which gives us new birth and new life, is worked by the Holy Spirit (v. 5). Paul argues that the Holy Spirit is not just the 'agent' or the 'means' of conversion, but is the gift of God, a gift which is not offered partially, but entirely.

According to the New Testament, Christian hope is not an uncertain desire. It is an expectation based on a guarantee. In fact, the Holy Spirit is our guarantee (Gal. 4:5–7; Rom. 8:15–17, 23; Eph. 1:5, 14). The word 'guarantee' is even used by the Apostle in 2 Corinthians 5:5 "Now it is God who has made us for this very purpose [to have an eternal dwelling in heaven] and has given us the Spirit as a deposit, guaranteeing what is to come."

Our hope is not uncertain. Quite the opposite! Romans 5:5 states "And hope does not disappoint us, because God has poured out his love into our hearts by the Holy Spirit, whom he has given us."

Hence, the Christian waits with hope, but what is he waiting for? The Holy Spirit? No! He is waiting for the moment "the sons of God will be revealed" (Rom. 8:19). The Spirit is the 'firstfruits' of God (Rom. 8:23). If we are believers, we already have this first gift of God. According to Scripture, no Christian ought to believe anything more than Jesus Christ. Nothing, no experience can be more beautiful or more important than to receive Jesus as our Saviour! As Paul says in Romans 8:23, "we wait eagerly for our adoption as sons."

Ephesians 1:13–14

The ministry of the Spirit of God is clearly seen in this passage:

> 13 And you also were included in Christ when you heard the word of truth, the gospel of your salvation. Having believed, you were marked in him with a seal, the promised Holy Spirit, 14 who is a deposit guaranteeing our inheritance until the redemption of those who are God's possession—to the praise of his glory.

Our guide to the goal (our complete deliverance at the return of Christ) is the first of the gifts of God: his Spirit. It remains impossible to become or to be a Christian without him (Rom. 8:9).

Hence, this question arises, what more can we ask for if we are, by Jesus Christ, 'children of God', 'inheritors of the promise', assured of the love of God and 'possessors of the Spirit promised to all those who believe'? What are we missing?? The New Testament answers this question clearly: nothing!

1 Corinthians 12:3

Finally, notice the beginning of Paul's discussion about the gifts of the Spirit of God: "Therefore I tell you that no one who is speaking by the Spirit of God says, 'Jesus be cursed,' and no one can say, 'Jesus is Lord,' except by the Holy Spirit."

Paul qualifies and describes here the work *par excellence* of the Spirit. His fundamental task is to bring men and women to declare that 'Jesus is Lord'. Hence, the man or woman who confesses the Lord is experiencing that which is the most profound work of the Spirit. Here is the true power of the Spirit. All other miracles, whether they be 'tongues' or 'healings' pale in comparison to the power which can change and convert a person so that she says: "Not I, but you Jesus Christ, you are Lord!"

Before the Corinthians, Paul brings up the subject in this way: When you were still non-Christians, the goal of your religious experiences was a sort of ecstasy (for one's self). But now you are Christians and you experience the Holy Spirit in your lives in a tangible way. The proof is your desire to glorify Jesus Christ. It is the Spirit that drives you to say in words and deeds: "Jesus is Lord". The climax of the work of the Spirit of God is to bring honour to Christ. Then the gifts or 'charisms' of the Spirit, the graces given by the Spirit to bless us (not the individual, but the whole church) are offered so that everyone can declare: "Jesus Christ is Lord".

Paul is more precise in 1 Corinthians 14:1–3 when he states that the reason for which the Spirit gives these 'graces' or 'charisms'. He gives them so that the church and every person in the church can be edified.

Paul insists above all on the gifts that help Christians become adults in faith. Hence, according to him, the greatest expression of the life of the Spirit is found in the building up of each other. In speaking to each other (v. 3), we help our brothers and sisters move forward in faith. Paul brings attention particularly to the gifts of communication. He does not say that so-called extraordinary gifts have no place. He does not question the value of speaking in tongues. But, it is better to be able to edify one's brother or sister, and this gift is more useful (v. 5), than to speak only to God (v. 2). Which one, self-service or mutual edification, is the mark of the Corinthians? The desire of the Apostle Paul is to instruct the Charismatics of his time, the Corinthians, to become 'adult' believers. His approach is clearly centred on Christ and his strategy consists in "bringing all thoughts captive to Christ" (2 Cor. 10:1–6) and "to boast of what the Lord has accomplished."

In their spiritual comprehension, the Corinthians were preoccupied with what they considered 'remarkable' and 'powerful'. Their preoccupations were not shared by Paul. As long as the Corinthians believed they were more 'spiritual' because they had received certain manifestations of the Spirit that other Christians did not have, they remained 'children' and in grave spiritual danger. They risked receiving another 'Jesus', a more spectacular and miraculous 'Jesus' and a more profound and soul-filling 'Spirit'.

Paul desired to turn the Corinthians (and the Christian 'charismatics' of the 20th century) from a preoccupation with their own 'spirituality' and 'power' to the humble and patient work in the body of Christ. In other words, Paul's message spoken to charismatics (and the whole church!) is one of humility, of service and of love for the body of Christ. As Paul says in 2 Corinthians 12:10: "That is why, for Christ's sake, I delight in weaknesses, in insults, in hardships, in persecutions, in difficulties. For when I am weak, then I am strong."

CHAPTER SIXTEEN

"Remember the Days of Old"

DAVID CRAIG

*Huguenot service: St. Andrew's Church-
Toronto, October 27, 1985*

*In: Canada's Huguenot Heritage, ed. Michael Harrison.
Toronto: Huguenot Society of Canada, 1987*

[211] Remember: "Rappelle à ton souvenir les anciens jours, Passe en revue les années, génération par génération, Interroge ton père, et il te l'apprendra, Tes vieillards, et ils te le diront."

"Remember the days of old; consider the generations long past. Ask your father and he will tell you, your elders, and they will explain to you" (Deut. 32:7).

This week, one of my students at Institute Farel, the French-speaking Reformed Faculty of Theology in Quebec City, made a terrible confession. She said, "In High School I hated history, just dates, names and dullness!" But, fortunately for me, she continued: "But now history, especially reformation history, has come alive! Now I know who I am!"

We live in an impatient society. We demand an instant response from a computer, an instant image on the television screen. In our 'now' society of instant gratification we pay little attention to these wise biblical words: "Remember . . . remember the days of old . . . consider your generations long past . . . ask your elders." And really why should we? For our definition of history is all too often the one Henry Ford espoused, "Just one damn thing after another." No order, no cohesion, no purpose!

Yet our forebears knew and every Christian should know that to listen to history is to observe "the hand of God in the affairs of men." Many of us here today can trace our family tree back to these great witnesses of God's grace of the seventeenth century, the Huguenots.

Yet whether or not we have a visible linear link with the Huguenots, we who share their vital and dynamic faith have the duty and the profound privilege to 'remember.' And what is it that we remember? On 31 October 1517 a veritable spiritual bomb exploded in the heart of Europe. Martin Luther nailed his ninety-five theses on the door of his church at Wittenburg. We remember that! But how many of us remember the path by which Luther arrived at these deep convictions? At the age of twenty-two, seeking peace for his troubled soul, Luther entered the monastery at Erfurt. He needed to please God. He wanted to be saved. But what a task! How did a sinner please the all-[212] powerful, the majestic Lord of the Universe. He who inhabited eternity? How ever could he, Martin Luther, approach the risen, exalted Christ, who, enthroned in the majesty of the rainbow, grasped in his hand the mighty sword of righteous judgement? How could he, a poor monk, diminish the distance between himself and the all-powerful God?

The church had taught him that becoming a monk was the sure and certain way to gain merit before God, and so be saved. He needed to suppress the flesh—to save himself. Yet the nagging question that burdened his soul was, "How can I know when I have done enough to merit heaven? How can I be sure that God will accept me?" The church taught that her sacraments offered merit to the sinner; particularly, the sacrament of confession. Yet to be forgiven, one must confess all. No sin could be hidden. But how can I know when I've confessed everything? Perhaps I've forgotten something. How can I know?

The church taught that salvation came through union with God. The only condition was that one love God. Yet for Luther, the risen, glorified

Christ was his judge... and rightly so! How, O how can I love my Judge? And to his confessor he cried, "Love God! How can I love Him? I can't love Him! I hate Him!"

In the midst of his despair, his confessor, a very wise man, gave him an important task. He was first to study, and then to teach to theological students the book of Psalms and the epistle of Romans. It was here that the light of salvation dawned in his unhappy soul, here that Luther passed from darkness to light. Someone has said that God always uses certain 'means.' His 'means' are often people. And the man that God used to teach Luther was a Frenchman. That is why many historians suggest that the Reformation was a gift from the French to the entire world. I love to say that to my Scottish colleagues!

The Frenchman's name was Jacques Lefèvre d'Etaples, philosopher and theologian, professor at the Sorbonne. Lefèvre, who remained a Roman Catholic, had written a commentary on the Psalms. Luther used this commentary in his preparation for his classes. He had no doubt read the words Lefèvre had written in the preface: "The hour has come in which our Lord Jesus Christ—the only Son, He who is truth itself and life itself, desires that His gospel be preached clearly to the world. Salvation is not achieved by your merit or any work that you can do. It is all of Christ! You cannot save yourself. Christ must save you. The cross is not yours—it is His!"

Then as Luther studied the words of Psalm 22, words spoken by Jesus on the cross, the truth dawned upon him. "My God, my God, why have you forsaken me! Why are you so far from saving me?" [213] How can it be? Jesus, abandoned by God? Jesus, the glorious Judge, suffering and what's more, suffering for me! How can it be? The glorious Judge... Victim... suffering... for me.

My friends, here is the beginning of the Reformation. Here is where it began for Luther—in the depths of his soul. His Judge became his Saviour and His Saviour made him free. And if we remember anything today, as Huguenots, we must remember this. For it is in the joy of knowing personally that God forgives us, that He, who is our judge, has become our Saviour, that every personal and individual reformation begins.

But that is just the beginning. As Huguenots, we remember also the cost ... the very high cost of reforming the church. For Luther it meant excommunication from the church he loved. Never did he condemn the church—he condemned the Papacy. He stated the final authority in the church must be the Word of God and not the word of man. But for him the church was holy, apostolic, catholic (that is universal) and the Body of Christ. "The church is the Lord's possession!" he cried. It is important then as Huguenots never to accept, even unconsciously, the idea that Luther separated from the church. Luther and Calvin and the other reformers, did not want to leave. They were excommunicated. They had no conception as two churches. They believed in one Holy, Catholic and apostolic church.

Pierre Courthial, dean of the Reformed Faculty of Theology in Aix-en-Provence, mentioned a conversation he had with a very good friend, a priest in the Roman Catholic Church. They had shared in worship on several occasions and the priest had a high regard for the Reformed faith and piety and he said to Courthial. "It is truly a pity that you are separated brothers." Pierre Courtial looked at him with astonishment and said, "Separated brothers! No my friend, we were driven out!" The reformers wanted reformation, not schism. They did not split the church. Their love and regard for the Body of Christ was far too profound for that. Division came by excommunication.

We remember too the vacillations of Francis the First, King of France. Francis claimed to have embraced the Reformation. Yet in order to appease the unreformed branch of the church, he issued orders for the arrest of 150 "religionnaires-calivinists." Eighteen had their tongues cut out. Twenty-seven, one per day, were burned alive over a slow fire. Another thirty-nine, those were called "pestiforous Lutherans," were burned alive in one day facing the Notre-Dame-de-Paris.

Yet we remember the wise and gracious words of the young John Calvin speaking to Francis in the first edition of the *Institutes* in August of 1535. [214] "My purpose," he states, in writing the *Institutes*, "was to transmit, especially to our French countrymen, of whom many hunger and thirst for Christ, the rudiments of faith in Him." Calvin pleads for the king's protection of the persecuted evangelicals, later called Protestants, who are "most loyal and worthy citizens." He speaks to the king of the necessity of Scripture being the final authority in the church and warns him of condemning innocent people on false charges, "for the innocent await Divine Vindication."

We remember the years of unrelenting persecution, of the minutely planned massacre on the evening of St. Bartholomew's Day when Charles IX ordered that not only Admiral Coligny, but every Huguenot within the realm be put to death—more than ten thousand in Paris alone, and throughout France from eighty to ninety-five thousand.

But we remember, too, the sins of our fathers, responding to violence with violence, and killing forty priests in the city of Nimes.

We remember those who were condemned and chained as galley slaves because of their faith and the prayer of one: "Fais seigneur que je regarde l'anneau de fer que je porte comme un anneau nuptial—et les chaines que je traine commes des chaines de ton amour."[1]

We remember that after such persecution the joy and hope that was brought by the Edict of Nantes in 1598. Henry IV declared this act perpetual and irrevocable. No one was to be arrested or persecuted for religious reasons. Reformed Christians were to have free access to all public offices. They were to be free to worship publicly in their own buildings. They could call and participate in Synods and General Assemblies and they could open and maintain schools. A new day of freedom had dawned . . . or had it?

This year [1985] marks the three hundredth anniversary of the revocation of the Edict of Nantes. Louis XIV, encouraged by the Roman Catholic hierarchy, began to exclude Protestants from certain positions. Several churches were destroyed. Synods were forbidden and

---

1. "Help me Lord to consider this iron ring that I wear as a wedding ring—and the chains that I carry as the bonds of your love."

special funds were made available for any Protestant who would reconvert to Catholicism. Finally, Louis sent into the towns and villages what he called his "booted missionaries"—his dragoons—to hunt down and convert by force or kill any Reformed Christian they could find. Finally, at Fontainebleau in 1685, the King declared the Edict of Nantes null and void. All Protestant churches were to be demolished, no services were to be held and all pastors had but fifteen days to leave the country. All children were to be baptized and raised in the Roman Catholic faith. Thus began a catastrophe from which France had never fully recovered. Our spiritual forebears left by the thousands. Switzerland, Holland, [215] England, Scotland, Ireland, South Africa, North America, South America and parts of Eastern Europe became their countries of refuge. They went everywhere seeking peace and a country they could call their own.

Those that could not escape were imprisoned or killed. Men were sent to the galleys, women to prison. Marie Durand spent thirty-eight years in the Tower of Constance for her faith. Bibles and Psalm books were hidden in false floors in country homes. Services were held secretly in small family groups. Baptisms, marriages and communion were celebrated all in one service, under the stars, with guards posted to warn the worshippers of danger.

Portable pulpits and collapsible communion cups were carried to the services. Bibles, starting with Exodus rather than Genesis, were used because Louis' soldiers had orders to burn all Bibles and Bibles, they knew, started with Genesis.

Yes, we remember these things, we remember that the first citizens of New France, our own Quebec, were refugees of religious persecution in France; that Louis Hébert, our first farmer, a Roman Catholic, sought a priest to baptize his nephew, but found none. He was obliged to ask a pastor to celebrate the baptism.

We remember that the first thirty-eight years of life in New France were dominated by the Huguenot presence, with Huguenot governors, Huguenot businessmen and Huguenot citizens.

"Remember the days of old . . . Rappelle à ton souvenir les anciens jours, Passe en revue les années, génération par génération . . . " Why remember: Because God is in it! We remember . . . and so know who we are. Yet what do we remember when all is said and done?

Surely it's the greatness of God, who preserved this, His people, in spite of terrible persecution, and has caused them to prosper. The writer of Deuteronomy 32 says this in verse 4: "O praise the greatness of our God. He is the Rock on which we are built. His work is perfect." Then in verse 9: "For the Lord's portion is His people. He found them in a desert land, He encircled them and cared for them. He guarded them as the pupil of His eye."

What do we remember? Surely it is the transforming power of the gospel of Christ that enlivens a man or a woman, strengthens him, strengthens her, to face the greatest trial with confidence and peace.

[216] What do we remember? We remember that tyranny, whether secular or religious, can never ultimately be victorious. In the city of Anduze, in the midi of France, the barracks that once housed Louis XIV's dragoons is now a Reformed church residence and conference centre.

What do we remember? We remember that God is faithful . . . faithful to His own Word, and nothing, no puny force of man, can obstruct or stay His hand.

Remember on this 300th anniversary of the Revocation of the Edict of Nantes that Louis XIV and those who opposed the Reformation of the church, lost! They are gone! But the Reform thrives. The church they fought for lives and has spread around the world to every land.

"I will proclaim the name of the Lord. Oh praise the greatness of our God, He is the Rock!" (Deut. 32:3–4)

Soli Deo Gloria.
Amen.

CHAPTER SEVENTEEN

"An Interview with David Craig"[1]

Channels (1988)

The following quote is from the report of the Special Committee to the 114th General Assembly in June 1988. Hopefully, this will provide some context for the interview with David Craig.

"In seeking to bring forward recommendations to the 114th General Assembly which would become our response to the matters brought forward by the Synod of Quebec and Eastern Ontario, the Committee has been guided by certain fundamental presuppositions. As The Presbyterian Church in Canada we must be the Presbyterian Church in every part of Canada. It is not open to us to deal with our francophone work in Quebec as if it were a foreign mission field, or to draw back from our mandate to minister to every part of our country in one or the other of our two official languages.

"Even more fundamentally, our reformed polity does not give congregations the possibility of withdrawing from The Presbyterian Church in Canada. Individuals may transfer their membership from our church to another, or to a new denomination. Indeed, we may have cordial relations with such a new denomination, but we cannot divest

---

1. [Rev. Dr. John Vissers, an active participant in the Renewal Fellowship, was the one who interviewed David on this occasion.]

part of our membership, property and mission in the way suggested. Clearly, we are called to a more creative francophone mission strategy which takes account of both linguistic and cultural issues, as well as theological issues.

"We would therefore make the following recommendations:

Recommendation No. 1
That the following principles be affirmed:
All are called to gospel obedience to the courts of the Church.
All are encouraged to associate cooperatively with any group or church with common goals for the sharing of the gospel.
Any communicant member may request a transfer of membership to any other denomination.
Any minister may request a letter of standing and lodge it with another denomination.
All courts of the Church and national boards of The Presbyterian Church in Canada are called to a continuing sensitivity of, pastoral caring for and outreach to and with the francophone community.

Recommendation No. 2
That we affirm the need for a francophone mission strategy that is Reformed, evangelical and ecumenical, requiring the initiative of the Board of World Mission in consultation with the Synod of Quebec and Eastern Ontario; a strategy which recognizes the need for self direction and creativity and including all francophone elements in our country.

Recommendation No.3
That the Board of World Mission report to the 115th General Assembly in terms of the development of such a francophone mission strategy, outreach policy and funding."

All three recommendations were adopted.

AN INTERVIEW WITH DAVID CRAIG

Channels:
We need to know something of your background and Nancy's background within the Presbyterian Church in Canada. Would you share some of that with us?

Craig:
I was ordained in 1966 within the Presbytery of Quebec. Immediately after ordination, Nancy and I went through missionary orientation in the Presbyterian Church in Canada and then in Nigeria. While in Nigeria I was involved in eldership training and pastoral work. Nancy was involved in teaching French.

Due to the Biafran situation many things became difficult and the women and children had to leave and the men remained. I was arrested and before the firing squad three times and finally released around 1968.

Upon returning to Canada I went to work with Ian Rennie in Fairview Church, Vancouver. After some persistence by the mission board, I returned to Nigeria although I had planned to do some doctoral work at Neuchâtel.

I remained in Nigeria for six months until someone was found to replace me and then went on to Neufchatel for doctoral work. The first two years were spent learning French as well as beginning my research and acting as chaplain at the University.

In 1976 I went to *L'Église St-Marc*, Quebec City as pastor of the congregation there and remained for eight years. In 1984 there was a Bible study in Trois-Rivières that needed further direction so Nancy and I felt called to go there. Francois Cordey, the first graduate of Institut Farel then became the pastor at *L'Église St-Marc*.

Channels:
What is your vision for a reformed and Presbyterian ministry in the province of Quebec?

Craig:

My vision goes back to the original vision of the French Canadian Missionary Society which our church inherited. The minutes of the French Canadian Missionary Society of 1860 reads as follows: "This society has no dearer object in view than to see this mission becoming gradually in its composition, management and support, purely and exclusively French Canadian. The committee repeats what has been formerly stated that in their belief, an earnest Protestant church, essentially French Canadian, free from the difficulties presented to their minds by the outward division of British churches, whilst combining all that is scriptural and doctrinal in practice, is the most fitted ecclesiastical organization for the French Canadian people." This statement was restated in 1874.

When our church inherited the mission society we received also the goal and vision that went along with it, which our church has lost sight of. The ERQ is not something new but something that is in continuity with the original vision of our work in Quebec.

This vision as I see it today is significant in that three reformed bodies are involved in it: the Christian Reformed Church of North America, the Presbyterian Church of America and the Presbyterian Church in Canada.

When Nancy and I came to Quebec there were three francophone Presbyterian churches in the provinces. Since that time there has been growth not only on the part of the Presbyterian Church in Canada but also in the Christian Reformed Church and the Presbyterian Church of America. The Christian Reformed Church came to Quebec around '78 or '79 and their original vision was to set up Christian Reformed francophone churches. We approached them and through discussion it was felt that there could be a united reformed witness within the province rather than two or three reformed churches side-by-side, out of which the vision of the ERQ has come. The Presbyterian Church of America, although reluctant at first, also started to buy into this vision and finally put down on paper that they were committed to this.

AN INTERVIEW WITH DAVID CRAIG

Channels:
What will you do or what do you feel your position now is in light of the General Assembly's decision of June 1988?

Craig:
In light of the decision the General Assembly is saying "no" to the proposal of the ERQ in terms of the Presbyterian Church in Canada and their involvement. This means that the alternative is separate francophone work within the province of Quebec, work which would have to be created, for presently there is no work there but that of the ERQ. The exception to that might be Melbourne and St. Luke's in Montreal, but generally the denomination would be looking at new work again in light of this decision.

I am hoping that I will be able to maintain my credentials as a minister with the Presbyterian Church in Canada and be added to the appendix to the roll. I can understand some of the reasoning of—although not agree with—the denomination as to their reluctance to be involved, one having to do with the ordination of women. We have been unable to get the candidates for ministry from the francophone ministry ordained, like Francois Cordey and Guy Dubé because they don't want their conscience bound and they are not prepared to accept the ruling of the Presbyterian Church on that particular issue.

Channels:
Presbytery has also recently taken a position on this. What is the position of the Presbytery of Quebec?

Craig:
They have hard-lined it. The Presbytery has refused to accept the recommendation that the French workers be seconded to the ERQ by the Presbyterian Church in Canada. The Presbytery refused to give its blessing to the work of the ERQ.

On terms of buildings—the Presbytery has taken the position of wanting to keep all the property in buildings within the Presbyterian

Church in Canada and they are looking for a new pastor in *l'Église St-Marc*. The Presbytery refused to make all necessary financial arrangements that would have been necessary had the earlier recommendation been put in place.

Regarding the work in Trois-Rivières, which is presently under grant, there will be no grants for work or personnel. I have met with the Board of World Mission since the General Assembly and they did show some flexibility in trying to accommodate our situation in that they could work with recommendations that did go to the Presbytery. These recommendations were drawn up on consultation with the Board of World Mission, but no indication from the Ecumenical Relations Committee as yet.

Channels:
What would be your last words to the Presbyterian Church in Canada concerning Francophone Ministry, including the evangelical witness within the denomination and what it might be able to do?

Craig:
I am very disappointed that the denomination did not look seriously at this option and this proposal. I feel that they are going to lose out with the francophone ministry in Quebec in the long run. We are dealing with a grass roots situation; these are Quebecois and it is French people doing French work and not a French work being thrust upon them from outside. The average age of the people involved is 27 or 28 years old—young families and young people.

I would question the problem of vision that our church has had as long as 120 years ago—a vision that goes back that long. There is a conflict, with some opting for mission and some for institution, but the problem is that those who are opting for institution will not accommodate the mission aspect unless it is uniquely a Presbyterian institutional mission working within Quebec.

In conclusion I am making an appeal to all evangelical congregations within the denomination to support the ministry and mission of

ERQ both financially and with its prayer to see that the ministry will go forward.

The whole movement of this francophone ministry and mission is thoroughly evangelical and being led by evangelicals and grounded in a solid and classic expression of the reformed faith in the Westminster Confession of Faith, the Heidelberg Catechism and the Canons of Dordt.

Channels:
Your vision then, David, has been for a francophone ministry within Quebec that would involve the Presbyterian Church in Canada and you have no desire to withdraw or leave the denomination, but rather to involve the denomination in a forward looking mission amongst the French people, the Quebecois.

Craig:
That's correct.

CHAPTER EIGHTEEN

"The First Mark of the Church"[1]

A SERMON BY DAVID CRAIG

Texts cited: John 15: 10–11, Philippians 4:4, John 17:13, 1 John 1:3–4

This morning we are starting a mini-series on the marks of the church, the marks that Jesus said ought to distinguish us as the church of the Lord.

By what marks ought we to be distinguished? What is the very first of these marks?

I think that if someone were have to asked me this question a few years ago, I would have answered that the most important is biblical doctrine, faithfulness to the Word of God! After this I would have noted holiness (that is, a holy life) and unity. Finally, love.

But in studying the New Testament and particularly the Gospel of John, I have come to a different conclusion. Here in John 17:13, as in other places, Jesus notes that the first mark of Christians is joy! I am not saying that holiness, unity and love are not important. Quite the contrary! Yet here the Lord begins with joy. So, the first mark of the church and, therefore, the most important is joy.

---

1. Sermon 19.

What is the first thing that we see in a new Christian? It is joy! We hear them say: "I feel great! I am happy and at peace." Yet most of us do not consider joy as a distinguishing characteristic of the church! Perhaps this shows us how far we are away from the spirit of the early church!

Ignatius, an early church leader said, "It is with joy that I would die for the Lord." Polycarp, another early church leader and disciple of the Apostle John, said this before Roman persecutors: "For 86 years I have served the Lord with joy. How could I now renounce my King who saved me?" Finally, Justin Martyr wrote early in the second century, "On the day which we call the day of the Sun (Sunday), all the faithful of the city and the countryside come together with great joy to listen to the writings of the apostles and prophets . . . and to praise the Lord." By these comments we can learn that a major distinguishing mark of the first Christians was joy!

The New Testament is a book of joy. In Greek the verb to rejoice is found more than 70 times. The noun is found around 60 times. Often we find it at the heart of messages. For example, the angel who announced the birth of Christ said, "I bring you good news of great joy that will be for all the people. Today in the town of David a Savior has been born to you; he is Christ the Lord" (Luke 2:10–11). Jesus said in John 15:11: "I have told you this so that my joy may be in you and that your joy may be complete." Jesus had just promised great things. Hence, the joy of which he spoke is the joy that fills the life of the Christian! James begins his letter, "Consider it pure joy, my brothers, whenever you face trials of many kinds, because you know that the testing of your faith develops perseverance" (James 1:2–3). Paul tells the Philippians, "Rejoice in the Lord always. I will say it again: Rejoice!" (Philippians 4:4).

One Scottish commentator, William Barclay, said, "the cry—may joy be with you—resounds throughout the New Testament! For, there is no Christianity of any quantity that is not animated by joy!" Hence, the Christian life that does not have joy is not a Christian life.

But the church of today, is it a joyous church? What do you think?

Without a doubt, we are all happier than we would be if we were not Christian. But when our worship leaders lead the worship service, what do they see on our faces? Joy? Peace? What do our song leaders see when they lead our singing? Joy? The desire to praise the Lord? Contentment to be in the Lord's presence? Do we long to pray aloud? Or is it always the same people who pray for everyone else? Do we come before the Lord with joy or out of obligation? Is the worship celebration a *celebration*? A *real* celebration?

No doubt we all agree that joy ought ideally to characterize the church and that this will be a reality in heaven. But what about down here?

Are our unhappy faces from family troubles? From daily tensions that we bring with us to church on Sunday morning?

In a Scottish church, there was one person who was clearly bored with the sermon so he began to doodle on the bulletin. Then he tried his hand at poetry and wrote this: "To live in heaven with the saints that will be glorious! But to live here on earth with the saints that is another story!" We know who we ought to be, but life, relations and circumstances, depress us and get in our way.

Is there a remedy? Is there a possible cure?

Look at John 17:13 and ask yourselves this question: "Why does Jesus pray for his joy to be in his disciples?" Is it not because he clearly sees the need? He sees that his disciples, like you and me, are often in danger of losing their joy.

So, he prays for them. Look at his first remedy for the absence of joy: "I am coming to you now, but I say these things while I am still in the world, so that they may have the full measure of my joy within them." What things does he say? The remedy, of course.

The first remedy of Jesus for our lack of joy is sound teaching. He teaches us. If we want joy, we have to come to know the Lord, to read his Word, to speak to him in prayer. This is the reason for which we put an emphasis on a time for each family to be in the Word every day, to pray together. This is the first remedy of our Lord. Like David, in

Psalm 19:8, we can say, "The precepts of the LORD are right, giving joy to the heart."

Jesus also says in John 15:10-11, "If you obey my commands, you will remain in my love, just as I have obeyed my Father's commands and remain in his love. I have told you this so that my joy may be in you and that your joy may be complete."

Psalm 34:9 tells us the same thing: "Taste and see that the LORD is good; blessed [joyful] is the man who takes refuge in him."

This is the first remedy for a lack of joy: to be focused on him; to be sure of him; to have all our thoughts fixed on him.

Fanny Crosby, a writer of more than 100 hymns, became blind at the age of five. She lived to be 95 years old, so, 90 years in blindness. She wrote these telling lines, "O, how happy am I! Even though I cannot see! I decided, in this world, I would live in contentment. See how many benedictions I have that others do not! Should I cry and be bitter because I cannot see? No. Impossible. I will not do it."

Someone might say, "But you don't know my life. I am 37, not married, my parents have died and I am alone. How will I live like this another 30 or 40 years?" Another could say, "I am tied to my wheelchair. My movements are so limited, my life is so hard." Maybe another will say, "After 36 years, my husband left me. I am alone. My life is too difficult. How do you except me to have joy? My circumstances don't allow it . . ."

Do you know what the word 'circumstances' actually means? It comes from two Latin words: *circum* which means around and *stare* which means to stand. Hence, circumstances are those things which stand around us. They are outside of who we really are. But where is the Lord? He is in us!

Hence, if we have Christ in us, within us, why are we so troubled by things which are outside of us? By our *circumstances*?

Here is the true secret to joy: the joy of the Lord lives within us!

Note here the second remedy that Jesus gives for a lack of joy. The first was a living relationship with the Lord, a vertical relation, if you will. But the second relation is one which is horizontal. This is that which we are trying to encourage with our *Groupes V.I.E.* If there is no horizontal communion, John says that we cannot be Christians.

John says in another place, "Whoever loves his brother lives in the light, and there is nothing in him to make him stumble. But whoever hates his brother is in the darkness and walks around in the darkness; he does not know where he is going, because the darkness has blinded him" (1 John 2:10–11). A relationship with God necessarily means that we have a relationship with his people. It is impossible to have the one without the other. Paul also speaks of a body with all its members (1 Cor. 12, for example).

John says, "We proclaim to you what we have seen and heard, so that you also may have fellowship with us. And our fellowship is with the Father and with his Son, Jesus Christ. We write this to make our joy complete" (1 John 1:3-4). If we lack joy, might it be possible that it is because we have cut off our relationship with other Christians?

We imagine that we might be able to form our own private network of people who think like us, but the Bible tells us that we need all other Christians and they need us. Without them God's communion will disappear, along with our joy.

Finally, the third remedy for a lack of joy is a life of obedience. Our sin separates us from God and from others.

Look at John 17:13. Jesus speaks of our lack of joy and immediately, in 17:15, prays that we be guarded from the Evil one. Verse 16: "They are not of the world, even as I am not of it." Verse 17: "Sanctify them by the truth; your word is truth." Do you see what he is saying? Jesus is praying that his disciples will be holy. Holy means 'set apart' for God.

Paul says the same thing in Romans 14:17–18: "For the kingdom of God is not a matter of eating and drinking, but of righteousness, peace and joy in the Holy Spirit, because anyone who serves Christ in this way is pleasing to God and approved by men." Many people do not have joy because they do not have what Paul is talking about.

These people do not rest in God or their conscience is very disturbed. They lack joy because they do not live an obedient life. They mark their own path instead of following the path of the Lord. They disobey his commandments.

Here, then, are the remedies of Jesus. This is his recipe for a life full of joy:

i. Eyes and heart fixed on the Lord and his Word.

ii. A close relationship with the people of God in his church.

iii. A life which puts in practice that which God wants: an obedient life.

May the Lord help us establish these three things in our own lives and the lives of our families. Some words of Paul, a magnificent promise, ought to accompany us all the days of our lives: "What, then, shall we say in response to this? If God is for us, who can be against us? He who did not spare his own Son, but gave him up for us all—how will he not also, along with him, graciously give us all things?" (Rom. 8:31–32).

God's Son Jesus prays for us right now—he prays that we be a joyful people!

Amen.

Bibliography

1. Primary Sources

1.1. Manuscript

Archives of Farel Faculté de théologie réformée (Montreal, Qc.)
—Lecture notes, 1978–2001

Archives of the Eglise réformée St-Paul (Repentigny, Qc.)
  i. Sunday Bulletins
  —Eglise Catholique Réformée St-Marc de Québec (1976–1984)
  —Eglise Catholique Réformée St-Matthieu de Trois-Rivières (1984–1994)
  —Eglise Réformée St-Paul de Repentigny (1994–2001)
  ii. Sermons
  —En français—1-797
  —In English—E1-E102
  iii. Bible/Topical Studies, Papers, Notes, Photocopies

Archives of the Presbytery of Montreal at The Presbyterian College (Montreal, Qc.)

i. "Église présbyterienne St-Luc, Ministère francophone, 1986- 90."
ii. "St.Andrew's, St. Lambert, 1950–64, G.C. Dalzell"
iii. "St.Andrew's, St. Lambert, 1965–83"

Personal Collection of Mrs. Nancy Craig (Repentigny, Qc.)

i. Letters and Personal Documents [including annual circular letters written for family and friends], 1967-2001
ii. Photos and other memorabilia

The Presbyterian Church in Canada Records and Archives Office (Toronto, On.)

i. G.B.M/B.W.M. Foreign Missions Collection—Presbyterian Church of Nigeria—File #103-G-3—"Personnel: Craig, David, 1966–1970".
ii. G.B.M./B.W.M. Administrative Records—Mission Education Director's Correspondence—File #1988-1003-80-1—"Deputation: David Craig, 1976–1968".
iii. G.B.M./B.W.M. Administrative Records—Mission Education Director's Correspondence—File #1988-1003-80-5—"Deputation Guidelines, 1967".
iv. E.H. Johnson fonds - File #1990-5007-5-2 —"Personnel: Rev. David Craig, 1968".

1.2. Bibliography of David Craig

"450 ans d'Histoire et une bougie pour les Eglises Réformées du Québec." *Le Christianisme au XXe siècle* 231 (4 Nov. 1989): 8–9.

BIBLIOGRAPHY

Bulletin Paroissial de l'Église Réformée St-Paul de Repentigny (later: *La Source*)
    "Mot du Pasteur." 2 (Apr. 2000): 1.
    "Mot du Pasteur." 5 (Jan. 2001): 1–2.
    "Deux mots d'un pasteur." 3 (Jun./Jul./Aug. 2000): 1–2.
    "Dieu se soucie des terroristes." 8 (Oct. 2001): 1–2.
    "Découragé?" 11 (Apr. 2003): 2–5.

Communiqué/Newsletter (Institut Farel/Farel Faculté de Théologie Réformée)
    "A Word from the President." (Spring/Summer 1993): 1–2.
    "The Lion King." (Spring 1995): 1, 4.
    "Of Conscience and Catholicity." (Fall 1995): 1, 3.
    "Test the spirits." (Fall 1996): 1–2.
    "Revive us again!" (Spring 1997): 1, 3
    "'Cur Deus Homo?' [Why God-Man?]" (Winter 1999): 1–2.

E.R.Q. Newsletter
    "Sola Gratia!" 2/2 (Spring 1996): 1–2.
    "Justice and Purity." 4/1 (Ice Storm 1998): 1–2.
    "Discerning the Faith." 6/2 (Fall 2000): 2–4.

Foundations
    "Hold Firmly to the Word." 2/2 (Fall 1981):

Nouvelles de l'E.R.Q. // En Lui
    May 1992
    Fall 1992
    "Mon troisième anniversaire de naissance." Special number
        (Mar. 2002): 1-2.

Parole. [David Craig, rédacteur en chef, 1985–86]
    "Les dons spirituels, [I]." 4/10 (1982): 3–6.
    "Les dons spirituels, II." 4/11 (1982): 14–18.

"Les dons spirituels, III." 4/12 (1982): 11–15.
"Les dons spirituels, IV." 5/13 (1983): 13–21.
"La promesse de Dieu à travers la Bible." 7/19 (1985): 4–7.
"La puissance de l'Esprit." 7/22 (1985): 18–22.
"Signe et Sceau du Salut." 8/25 (1986): 19–23.

Presbyterian College Life
"New Faces at P.C." (1964): 10–11
"Dialogue about Dialogue." (1965): 10–11.

The Presbyterian Record
"Operation Calabar: An Eye-Witness Account." (Dec. 1967): 2–3, 24–25.
"[De] Québec avec Amour." (Feb. 1978): 10–11.

La Vie Chrétienne
"Le sens du baptême." 26/8–9 (Aug.-Sept. 1977): 1–2.
"Méditation: Éphésiens 3: 20–21." (Oct.-Nov. 1986): 11.

[With Paulin Bédard] L'Eglise Réformée du Québec. [Unpublished manuscript. Québec, 1988.]

"Pour établir le statut légal du foetus." [In section 'votre opinion'] [*Le nouvelliste?*], [March 1988?].

"Remember the days of old." In: *Canada's Huguenot Heritage: Proceedings of Commemorations held in Canada during 1985 of the Tercentenary of the Revocation of the Edict of Nantes.* Ed. Michael Harrison. Toronto: Huguenot Society of Canada,1987. 211–216.

BIBLIOGRAPHY

"Témoignage protestant au Québec." In : *Le Protestantisme au Québec: Hier, aujourd'hui et demain*. Textes du symposium organisé par le Sénat du Collège Presbytérien, 20–21 November 1981. Montreal: Presbyterian College, 1–9.

2. Newspaper and Magazine Articles, Unpublished Articles, Minutes[1]

Annett, Kenneth H. *Huguenot Influence in Quebec*. (Unpublished manuscript), [1977].

Boulanger, Jean-Marc et Line. "A la mémoire de David Trevor Craig, 1937–2001". Discours fait au nom de l'Eglise Réformée St-Paul pour l'enterrement de David Craig, 29 October 2007.

Bulletin Paroissial de l'Eglise Réformée St-Paul de Repentigny (later: *La Source*)

Christian Observer (26 Aug. 1988): 11.

"Cours de théologie protestante en français, au Québec." *Dimanche-Matin* (19 Aug. 1979): 29.

Dolan-Caron, Rita, "La prémière exposition du Musée des Religions de Nicolet: Témoignages d'appréciation des spécialistes." *Le Nouvelliste* (3 Nov. 1986): 5.

Drennan, Ray. "View from the Mission field—Not mandated to convert." *The Presbyterian Record* (Feb. 1988): 6.

E.R.Q. Newsletter. [Various authors].

Gautier, Gérard. "French-Speaking Protestants Seek Their Own Mission In Their Own Society." Trans. Judy Quenneville. *The Observer* (Jul. 1982): 32–33.

———. "Les Protestants du Canada." *Le Christianisme au XXe siècle* [232?]: 4.

---

1. Many of the references in this section were found archival records as clippings or photocopies without complete bibliographic information. I have tried to provide as much missing information as possible, but certain authors, publishers, dates or page numbers were not possible to track down.

Gyselinck, Michele. "The seeds of the Reformed Church in Quebec have sprouted." *Christian Courier* (23 Jul. 1993): 10.

Harrison, Paul. "A New Lagos Landmark: A look at an unusual experiment in church design." *Interlink: The Nigerian-American Quarterly Magazine* 5/2 (Apr.-Jun. 1969): 2–3.

Hillen, Ernest. "The Longest Moment of David Craig: It changed him, he says, and if what he believed needed testing, it was tested then, facing the Nigerian rifles." *Weekend Magazine* 18/4 (27 Jan. 1968): 2–7.

Kallemeyn, Harold. "Reformed Theological Training in Quebec City?" *The Banner* (1 June 1981): 11.

Klinck, Steven A. "A 'missionary report' to the assemblies of Lennoxville and Huntingville." (Unpublished manuscript, Oct. 1970). 12 pp.

Légaré, Isabelle. "Au Musée des religions de Nicolet: la rencontre des croyances." *Le Nouvelliste* (31 Mar. 1993).

Marlowe, Jeff and Mischa. "The Africa Beat: News from Jeff and Mischa Marlowe." PCA Mission to the World, Dakar, Senegal Church Planting Team (June 1999).

Martin, David A. "Mennonite Fundamentalism and the Hawkesville Brethren: an examination of the origins of the Wallenstein Bible Chapel and its impact on the local Mennonite Community." *Waterloo Historical Society* 91 (2004).

McLelland, Joseph C. "View from the ivory tower." *Presbyterian Record* (Nov. 1987): 8–9.

Members and adherents of the Eglise St-Marc. "Letter to Presbytery of Quebec." (9 Nov. 1982).

Ministère francophone, consistoire du Québec [Daniel Forget, executive secretary]. "Rapport du Comité spécial sur la stratégie du Ministère francophone." (Jun. 1989).

Myanmar Presbyterian Community Church. *Combine[d] pastors and workers seminar—Conducted by Rev. David Craig.* Yangon. [Unpublished manuscript.]

"New denomination inaugurated in Quebec." *Faith Today* (Mar./Apr. 1989): 49.

Minutes of Meetings of The Presbyterian Church in Canada

BIBLIOGRAPHY

- —General Assembly
- —Synod of Quebec and Eastern Ontario
- —Presbytery of Montreal
- —Presbytery of Quebec

"Musée des Religions: Centre international d'exposition." *Le nouvelliste* (2 Aug. 1991): 1–20.

Paillé, Roland. "Le Dr Henry Morgentaler ne se voit pas comme un meurtrier 'nous sommes tous pro-vie'." *Le nouvelliste* 69/125 (27 Mar. 1989): 1.

""Quebec offers Protestants 'day of opportunity'," ministers says." [Quebec English-language daily—sometime in Nov. or Dec. 1976.]

Racine, Daniel. "La nouvelle réforme et le christianisme aujourd'hui." *Crédo* (Oct. 1975): 17–20.

"Reformed church planned for Quebec." *Calvinist Contact* (28 Mar 1980).

Roy, Michelle. "Le grand principe de l'Eglise catholique réformée: La primauté sur la bible plutôt que sur la tradition." *Le Nouvelliste* (5 May 1988): 36.

Stewart, K.J. "Conscience controversy dominates Presbyterian Assembly." *Calvinist Contact* (9 Jul. 1982).

"The 115th General Assembly, Montreal, June 4 to 9, 1989." *Presbyterian Record* (Jul.–Aug. 1989): 28.

Thompson, Bernard. "The importance of prayer: the foundation of a nation's history." *Navlog* 39/4 (International Edition—Oct. 1978): 3-6.

Yeung Mar, Carol J. "... And all these things done ... in his name." (Dec. 1991). [unpublished manuscript]

3. General Bibliography

Akak, Eyo Okon. *A Critique of Old Calabar History.* Calabar: Ikot Offiong Welfare Association, 1981.

Akpan, Ntieyong U. *The Struggle for Secession, 1966–1970: A Personal Account of the Nigerian Civil War.* London: Frank Cass, 1971.

Aye, Efiong U. *Old Calabar Through the Centuries.* Calabar: Hope Waddell Press, 1967.

Bédard, Marc-André. *Les Protestants en Nouvelle-France.* Québec: La Société Historique de Québec, 1978.

Bienvenue, Louise. *Quand la Jeunesse Entre en Scène: l'Action catholique avant la Révolution tranquille.* Montreal: Boréal, 2003.

Bierschock, Kurt P. *Zivilreligion, Ethnizität und soziale Strukturen: Zur Genese zivilreligiöser Phänomene in Québec während der dreißiger bis fünfziger Jahre.* Bochum: Universitätsverlag Dr. N. Brockmeyer, 1993.

Blackburn, Carole. *Harvest of Souls: The Jesuit Missions and Colonialism in North America 1632–1650.* Montreal and Kingston: McGill-Queen's University Press, 2000.

Burkinshaw, Robert. *Pilgrims in Lotus Land: Conservative Protstantism in British Columbia 1917–1981.* Kingston/Montreal: McGill-Queens University Press, 1995.

Butler, Jon. *The Huguenots in America: A Refugee People in New World Society.* Cambridge, Mass.: Harvard University Press, 1983.

Castel, Frédéric. "Progrès du catholicisme, influence de l'immigration: Les grandes tendances de l'affiliation religieuse depuis la Seconde Guerre Mondiale." In: *l'Annuaire du Québec 2004.* Ed. Michel Venne. Montreal: Fides, 2003. 273–282.

Červenka, Zdenek. *The Nigerian War 1967–1970.* Frankfurt am Main: Bernard & Graefe Verlag für Wehrwesen, 1971.

Clifford, N. Keith. *The Resistance to Church Union in Canada 1904–1939.* Vancouver: University of British Columbia Press, 1985.

Coad, F.R. *A History of the Brethren Movement: Its Origins, Its Worldwide Development and Its Significance for the Present Day.* Vancouver: Regent College Publishing, 2001.

Cramp, J.M. *Les Mémoires de Madame Feller: Avec une brève esquisse de la Mission de la Grande Ligne dans les années qui ont suivi.* St-Romuald, Québec: Editions Beauport, [1989?].

Cronje, Suzanne. *The World and Nigeria: The Diplomatic History of the Biafran War 1967–1970.* London: Sidgwick & Jackson, 1972.

Crowley, Terry. "The French Regime to 1760." In: *A Concise History of Christianity in Canada*, eds. Terrence Murphy and Roberto Perin. Toronto: Oxford University Press, 1996.

BIBLIOGRAPHY

Dickinson, John A. and Brian Young, *A Short History of Quebec*, 2nd ed. Toronto: Copp Clarck Pitman Ltd., 1993.

Federal Nigeria XI/13 (Aug. 1967).

Ferretti, Lucia. *Brève histoire de l'Eglise catholique au Québec*. Montreal: Boréal, 1999.

Gaudette, Michel. *Guerres de Religion d'Ici: Catholicisme et Protestantisme Face à l'Histoire*. Trois-Rivières: Editions Souffle de Vent, 2001.

Gauvreau, Michael. *The Catholic Origins of Quebec's Quiet Revolution, 1931–1970*. Montreal/Kingston: McGill-Queen's University Press, 2005.

Goldberger, Pierre. "Theological Reflections on the P.Q. Victory," *ARC Journal* 4/2 (Spring 1977): 22–36.

Hamelin, Jean. *Histoire du Catholicisme Québécois: Le XXe siècle*. Vol. III. Montreal: Boréal, 1984.

Hamilton, Thomas J. "Canadian Presbyterian Evangelism, 1925-1972." CD ROM.

Hardy, René. *Contrôle social et mutation de la culture religieuse au Québec 1830–1939*. Montreal: Boréal, 1999.

Hentsch, Thierry. *Face au Blocus: La Croix-Rouge internationales dans le Nigéria en guerre (1967–1970)*. Geneva: Institut Universitaire de hautes études inernationales, 1973.

Johnston, Geoffrey. *Of God and Maxim Guns: Presbyterianism in Nigeria, 1846–1966*. Waterloo, Ont.: Wilfred Laurier University Press, 1988.

Johnston, John Alexander. "Edward Hewlett Johnson: Internationalist and Man of Peace." In: *Called to Witness: Profiles of Canadian Presbyterians. A Supplement to Enduring Witness*. Vol. 3. Ed. John S. Moir. Hamilton: Committe on History, The Presbyterian Church in Canada, 99–110.

Kim, Andrew E. "The Absence of Pan-Canadian Civil Religion: Plurality, Duality, and Conflict in Symbols of Canadian Culture." *Sociology of Religion*. 54/3 (1993): 257–275.

Kirk-Greene, A.H.M. *Crisis and Conflict in Nigeria: A Documentary Sourcebook 1966-1969*. London: Oxford University Press, 1971.

Labelle, Gilles. "Sens et destin de la colère antithéologique au Québec après la révolution tranquille." In: *Diversité et identités au Québec et dans les régions d'Europe.* Eds. Jacques Palard, Alain-G. Gagnon, Bernard Gagnon. Quebec: Les Presses de l'Université Laval, 2006. 337–364.

Lacoursière, Jacques. *Histoire Populaire du Québec,* Vol. 1. Sillery, Quebec: Septentrion, 1995.

———. *Une Histoire du Québec.* Sillery, Quebec: Septentrion, 2002.

Lacroix, Benoît. *La foi de ma mère: La religion de mon père.* Montreal: Bellarmin, 2002.

Lalonde, Jean-Louis. *Belle-Rivière, 1840–2006.* Montreal: Société d'histoire du protestantisme franco-québécois, 2007.

———. *Des loups dans la bergerie: les protestants de langue française au Québec. 1534–2000.* Montreal: Fides, 2002.

Lamonde, Yvan. *Histoire sociale des idées au Québec 1896–1929.* Montreal: Fides, 2004.

Larin, Robert. *Brève histoire des protestants en Nouvelle-France et au Québec.* Saint-Alphonse-de-Granby, Quebec: Editions de la Paix, 1998.

Legaré, Francine. *Samuel de Champlain: Father of New France.* Montreal: XYZ Publishing, 2004.

Lougheed, Richard. *La Conversion Controversée de Charles Chiniquy.* Quebec: La Clarière, 1999.

Lougheed, Richard, Wesley Peach and Glenn Smith, eds. *Histoire du Protestantisme au Québec depuis 1960: Une Analyse Anthropologique, Culturelle et Historique.* Quebec: La Clarière, 1999.

Lucas, Sean. *On Being Presbyterian: Our Beliefs, Practices, and Stories.* Phillipsburg, New Jersey: P&R Publishing, 2006.

MacLeod, A. Donald. *C. Stacey Woods and the Evangelical Rediscovery of the University.* Downers Grove, Il.: IVP Academic, 2007.

Markell, H. Keith. *History of The Presbyterian College, Montreal. 1865–1986.* Montreal: The Presbyterian College, 1987.

McFarlan, Donald M. *Calabar: The Church of Scotland Mission Founded 1846.* Rev. ed. London: Thomas Nelson and Sons, 1957.

BIBLIOGRAPHY

McLelland, Joseph C. *Understanding the Faith: Essays in Philosophical Theology*. Presbyterian College Studies in Theology and Ministry, Vol. 1. Toronto: Clements Academic, 2007.

McNab, John. "Our Overseas Adventures." In: *Essays on Presbyterianism in Canada*. Ed. Centennial Committee of The Presbyterian Church in Canada. Toronto: Presbyterian Publications, 1966. 83–110.

Moessner, Jeanne Stevenson. "Missionary Motivation." *Sociological Analysis* 53/2 (1992): 189–201.

Moir, John S. *A History of Biblical Studies in Canada: A Sense of Proportion*. Chico, Ca.: Scholars Press, 1982.

———. *Christianity in Canada: Historical Essays*. Ed. Paul Laverdure. Yorkton, SK: Redeemer's Voice Press, 2002.

———. *Enduring Witness: A History of the Presbyterian Church in Canada*. Don Mills, Ont.: Presbyterian Church in Canada, 2004.

Murphy, Terrence and Roberto Perin. *A Concise History of Christianity in Canada*. Toronto: Oxford University Press, 1996.

Paquin, René. "Les protestants canadiens-français et le 'réveil' catholique dans le Québec du XIXe siècle: brève histoire d'une concurrence." In *L'identité des protestants francophones au Québec: 1834–1997*. Ed. Remon, Denis. Montreal: Acfas, 1998.

Peach, Wesley. "Rethinking Revival in Québec." In: *Transforming Our Nation: Empowering the Canadian Church for a Greater Harvest*. Ed. Murry Moerman. Richmond, B.C.: Church Leadership Library, 1998. 173–202.

Piché, Lucie. *Femmes et changement social au Québec: L'apport de la Jeunesse ouvrière catholique féminine, 1931–1966*. Quebec: Les Presses de l'Université Laval, 2003.

Piepkorn, Arthur Carl. "Plymouth Brethren (Christian Brethren)." *Concordia Theological Monthly* 41 (1970): 165.

Randall, Catherine. "Une Fille et la Parole: Le Protestantisme Canadien-français d'Henriette Feller," In: *L'identité des protestants francophones au Québec: 1834–1997*. Ed. Denis Remon. Montreal: Acfas, 1998. 53–73.

Rawlyk, George A. *The Canadian Protestant Experience. 1760–1990*. Burlington, On.: Welch Publishing Company Inc., 1990.

Remon, Denis, ed. *L'identité des protestants francophones au Québec: 1834–1997.* Montreal: Acfas, 1998.

Rennie, Ian. "Conservatism in the Presbyterian Church in Canada in 1925 and beyond: an introductory exploration," *The Canadian Society of Presbyterian History Papers* (1982): 29–59.

Rousseau, Louis et Fédéric Castel. "Un défi de la recomposition identitaire au Québec: le nouveau pluralisme religieux." In: *Diversité et identités au Québec et dans les régions d'Europe.* Eds. Jacques Palard, Alain-G. Gagnon and Bernard Gagnon. Quebec: Les Presses de l'Université Laval, 2006. 251–280.

Routhier, Gilles. "Quelle Sécularisation? L'Eglise du Québec et la modernité." In: *Religion, sécularisation, modernité : Les expériences francophones en Amérique du Nord.* Ed. Brigitte Caulier. Quebec: Les Presses de l'Université Laval, 1996. 73–96.

Savard, Pierre. *Aspects du Catholicisme canadien-français au XIXe siècle.* Montreal: Fides, 1980.

Smith, Glenn, "The Québec Protestant Church." In: *Transforming Our Nation: Empowering the Canadian Church for a Greater Harvest.* Ed. Murry Moerman. Richmond, B.C.: Church Leadership Library, 1998. 203–268.

Somers, David. "Lutheran Missionary Activity Among Quebec Francophones in the Late-Twentieth Century," In: *Historical Papers 1993. Canadian Society of Church History.* Ed. Bruce L. Guenther (1993): 248–259.

Strout, Richard E. "The Latter Years of the Board of French Evangelization of the Presbyterian Church in Canada, 1895–1912." M.A. thesis, Bishop's University, 1986.

The Maiden Visit of Governor Esuene: An Account of the first official visit of His Excellency Colonel U.J. Esuene, Military Governor of South-Eastern State, to Calabar after the liberation of the town. [No Place]: Department of Information, South Eastern State of Nigeria, Calabar; Ministry of Home Affairs and Information, 1968.

Trudel, Marcel. *Chiniquy.* Trois-Rivières: Editions du Bien Public, 1955.

———. *Histoire de la Nouvelle France.* Vol. 1. Montreal: Fides, 1963.

BIBLIOGRAPHY

———. *Initiation à la Nouvelle-France: histoire et institutions*. Montreal: Holt, Rinehart, et Winston, Ltd, 1968.

Vaudry, John. *Built on the Rock: A History of Cote des Neiges Presbyterian Church, Montreal*. Montreal: 2008.

Vissers, John. *The Neo-Orthodox Theology of W.W. Bryden*. Eugene, Or.: Pickwick Publications, 2006.

Voisine, Nive. "L'ultramontains canadiens-français au XIXe siècle," In: *Les Ultra-montains canadiens-français*. Eds. Nive Voisine et Jean Hamelin. Montreal: Boréal Express, 1985. 67-104.

Vogt-Raguy, Dominique. "Les communautés protestants francophones au Québec. 1834–1925." Ph.D diss., l'Université Michel de Montaigne—Bordeaux III, 1996.

Walsh, H.H. *The Christian Church in Canada*. Toronto: The Ryerson Press, 1956.

Watson, J. Ralph. *Protestants in Montreal. 1760–1992*. Hantsport, N.S.: Printed by Lancelot Press, 1992.

Zuidema, Jason. "Marginalisation et 'raison d'être' du Chrétien Réformé Francophone du Québec." *Revue Farel* 2 (2007): 1–19.

Index

Alliance Réformée Évangélique
  (A.R.E.), 89-90, 99-100
Ariège, René, 72
Augustine, 162
Baie Comeau, 22-24
Barker, Ken, 23
Barrier act, 103-104
Barth, Karl, see Neo-Orthodoxy
Bédard, Paulin, 102
Bee-keeping, 5
Bethel Bible Institute, 26
Biafran conflict, 37-53
Bible study groups, 85, 97, 128,
  132-133, 205
Board of Missions, 3, 29-30, 37-38,
  55, 59-62, 63, 120
Brethrenism, 7, 8, 9, 12
Calabar, 31-51
Canadian Bible Society, 86
Catholicism, 18, 81, 84, 86, 94,
  127-128, 157-160, 169, 173-176
Channels, 107-108, 193
Chaplain in Army, 92-95
Chaplain, 74
Charismatic movement, 87, 179-184
Children of David and Nancy, 62,
  126-127
Christian Reformed Church, 100
Confessions, 143
Conseil des Églises Réformées du
  Québec (C.E.R.Q.), 84, 100-104
Conversion (Faith), 8
Cordey, François, 102
Courtial, Pierre, 182
Covenant theology, 147
Craig, Nancy, 24-27, 32, 34-35, 38,
  54, 56, 66, 70, 73, 76, 82, 85,
  96, 126-127
Cruvellier, Jean, 65, 80
Cuthbert Chapel, 137
David as Pastor, 128-129
Davidson, Ross, 81, 119
deBlois, Jean-Guy, 90
Deputation, 60-66
Divinity of Christ, 12, 21, 151-162
Dubé, Guy, 87
Eastern Orthodoxy, 74
Ecumenism, 18-19, 167-168
Edict of Nantes, 191
Education, 5, 9, 11-29, 71-74
Église Presbytérienne St-Luc (Montreal), 101-102
Église Réformée du Québec (E.R.Q.),
  101, 104, 106-109, 115-123,
  130, 196-199
Eramosa Gospel Hall, 6, 7

Evangelicalism, Evangelicals, 86-87, 105
Evangelism Explosion, 131
Evangelism, 157-58
Expo '67, 53-54, 56
Fairview Presbyterian Church, 66-68
Faith, 150
Family, 3-9, 14, 56
Farel Reformed Theological Seminary (Institut Farel), iv, 85, 91, 127, 135
Farel, Guillaume, 71-72, 151-152, 160
Forget, Daniel. 109-114, 116-117, 121
Foucachon, Francis, 129-130
Freedom in Christ, 154-156
French Canadian Missionary Society (19th century), 100, 122, 196
French language/missions, 6, 16, 22-23, 31, 65, 71, 83, 137, 158
Funeral, 135-138
Garneau, François-Xavier, 173
Geleynse, Martin, 81, 90
General Assembly, 91, 100-106, 108, 193
Guthrie, Frank, 6, 9
Hall, Ross, 56
Hill, Arthur, 25, 27, 92
Hillen, Ernest, 41
Holy Spirit, 157, 162, 179-184
Hope Waddell Training Institute, 31-37
Huguenots, 172-178, 186, 188-190
Hummelen, Remmelt, 66
InterVarsity Christian Fellowship, 12
Israel, 98
Jehovah's Witnesses, 23
Jesuits, 175
Johnson, E.H., 30, 37-38, 67

Jossinet, Armand, 80
Joy, 154-155, 201-206
Kendall, Ralph, 100, 102
Kettle, David, 116
Kirk, Mavis, 61
Klinck, Nancy, see Craig, Nancy
Kouwenberg, J. Hans, 106, 108
L'Abri, 74-76
La Vie Chrétienne, 101
Labrador City, 22
Lagos Presbyterian Church, see Lagos
Lagos, Nigeria, 31, 68-70
Lefèvre d'Etaples, Jacques 187
Liberalism, Liberal theologians, 19-21, 105, 143, 151-152
Loyalty oath, 117-119
Marlowe, Jeff, 133
Marriage, 164-165
McLean, Archie, 14
Membership, 98
Mezaour, Sadi, 81
Michaud, Patrice, 117, 119
Missionary method, 86
Montgomery, John Warwick, 12-13
Myanmar, 133
Navigators, 87
Neo-Orthodoxy, 20-21, 149-160
Neuchâtel, see Switzerland
New France, 173-177
Nigeria, 29-56
Nigeria, David's reflections on, 62-66
Ordination, 102-104, 161, 164
Parole magazine, 90
Patterson, Alison, 102
Porret, Jean, 95
Preaching, 13, 153-154, 157
Presbyterian Church in America,

INDEX

99-100
Presbyterianism, 12, 24
Presbytery of Quebec, 91, 109-119
Priestly, Sam, 100
Protestantism in Quebec, 79-80, 172-190
Quebec (*Église St-Marc*), 79-92, 103
Racine, Daniel, 90, 98
Ransom, Malcolm, 30, 60-61
Reader, Paul, 14
Reformation, 13, 73, 82, 83-84, 157-160, 186-188
Rennie, Ian, 67
Repentigny (*Église St-Paul*), 129
Resurrection, see Divinity of Christ
Revival, 80-82, 125
Révolution tranquille, 81, 88
Richmond (*Église St-Paul*), 81
Roberts, Earle, 30
Schaeffer, Francis, 74-76
Schindell, Kit (née Somerville), 68
Scott, Paul, 12
Scripture, 13, 74, 149-154
Seconding, 108, 120
Sparks, Doug and Sylvie, 88
St. Andrew's Presbyterian Church, St. Lambert, 22-24, 27
St-Georges-de-Beauce, 87, 99
Strout, Richard, 100
Switzerland, 71-78
Synod of Quebec and Eastern Ontario, 89, 91
Talbot, Rodger, 29, 31
The Church, 160-165
The Presbyterian Church in Canada, 15
The Presbyterian College, iv, 15-23, 29, 42, 171

The Presbyterian Record, 88
The Renewal Fellowship, 107
Thibault, Lise, 95, 136
Trois-Rivières (*Église St-Matthieu*), 3, 95-98, 125-129, 152-153
United Church of Canada, 16, 80, 101
Unity, 87, 90, 99-105, 133, 160, 163
Vaudry, John, 103
Vissers, John, 193
Walker, Blake, 108-109
Waterloo Lutheran University, 9, 11-15
Westminster Club, 12
World Religions Museum in Nicolet, 127-128
Youth and student work, 67, 74, 82, 95, 97, 131
Zoellner, Jean (Garnet), 88